Fishin' Around

OTHER BOOKS BY BURTON L. SPILLER

Thoroughbred
Firelight
Grouse Feathers
More Grouse Feathers
Northland Castaways
Drummer in the Woods

Burton L. Spiller

Fishin' Around

Illustrations by Milton C. Weiler

Foreword by H. G. Tapply

WINCHESTER PRESS

Library of Congress Catalog Card Number: 13-88872
ISBN: 0-87691-128-9

PUBLISHED BY WINCHESTER PRESS
460 PARK AVENUE, NEW YORK 10022

Printed in the United States of America

Contents

Foreword

It will come as a surprise to many to learn that Burton L. Spiller was a fisherman—not your Saturday-if-it-doesn't-rain kind of fisherman, but the devout and dedicated kind of fisherman who would be likely to write stories about fishing.

In his lifetime Burt enjoyed more fame than most, but no part of it accrued to him because he was a caster of flies. In the town of East Rochester, New Hampshire, where he lived during the last sixty-two years of his life, he was known mainly as a gladiolus farmer. No doubt his neighbors knew he liked to fish and hunt, as most everyone does in the country, and a few who were close to him surely knew he did some scribbling on the side—but still, when you thought of Burt Spiller you thought of gladiolus blooms and bulbs, and that is fame of a sort.

Away from East Rochester, in New York State and Pennsylvania and West Virginia, in Michigan and Wisconsin and wherever else the ruffed grouse is indigenous, Burt achieved fame of quite a different sort. Ever since the early '30s, till this very day, he has been known and revered as the country's preeminent writer of grouse stories and acknowledged dean of grouse hunters. If you were to ask any literate upland gunner to name the finest book ever written about hunting the ruffed grouse, chances are he would tell you it is Burton L. Spiller's *Grouse Feathers,* which was first published in 1935 by Derrydale Press and is still relished today in a modern edition released last year by Crown Publishers.

In all, Derrydale published four of Burt's books, mostly devoted to grouse and grouse dogs and grouse hunters. Later, Van Nostrand brought out *Drummer in the Woods,* a collection of Burt's grouse-shooting stories garnered from the pages of *Field & Stream* and other sporting magazines. He wrote with grace and humor and great sensitivity and has been called, with good reason, the poet laureate of grouse hunting. The good people of East Rochester, who thought of him as a grower of prize-winning gladioli, might be surprised to know how famous their townsman had become, for an entirely different reason, in other parts of the country.

Yet I first knew Burt as a fisherman. In later years we hunted grouse together—we had fourteen good seasons in the autumn uplands before age finally caught up with him—but in the beginning we went fishing. We trolled streamer flies on Sebago Lake for landlocked salmon and cast for trout on the Kennebago, Moose, Kennebec and a few other rivers, plus some remote ponds, in Maine, and on the Pine River in New Hampshire. I would say that in the spring of the year Burt was as enthusiastic about fishing as he was in the fall about hunting—and the stories he tells in this book will bear me out.

It would not be entirely correct to say that Burt was a highly skilled fisherman, and he certainly was not a sophisticated one. He had a casual attitude toward fishing and had nothing to do with such esoteric aspects of it as calibrating leader diameters or judging the action of a fly rod by its rate of vibration. He cast a fly well and played a trout deftly, but his attention was likely to wander if he heard the piping of a song sparrow, and I have seen him stop fishing altogether to sit and watch a muskrat that happened to blunder into his pool.

But I am telling you something you will discover soon enough for yourself when you read the pages that follow. Just don't expect to learn very much about how to catch fish; instead, learn how catching fish can be such a pleasant way to spend your time.

This book is published posthumously. Nearly all of the material was written in earlier times, and gathering the stories together in their proper sequence, and editing and revising the text, occupied my old friend during the last months allotted to him. Indeed, it may have prolonged his life, for he lived to see the completed manuscript shipped off to the publisher but, alas, not quite long enough to see the printed result of his last labor.

Burton Lowell Spiller, born in Portland, Maine, on December 21, 1886, died of the infirmities of age in Rochester, New Hampshire, on May 26, 1973. There were many sprays of gladioli at his services.

—H. G. TAPPLY

East Alton, New Hampshire
September 1973

Prologue: What Is a Fisherman?

THE WAYS OF A GENUINE, dyed-in-the-wool fly-fisherman are beyond human comprehension, but I have arrived at a few definite conclusions. Fishermen are a clan, a tightly knit organization governed by inflexible rules, and with a caste system as rigid as any ever practiced in India. The rajah, or high potentate, is a dry-fly purist who will offer the fish nothing more tangible than a microscopic bit of hair and feather tied in the erroneous belief that it imitates some sort of insect, but actually looks like nothing in the heavens above, the earth below, or the waters beneath the earth.

Anointed with a mystic concoction called dry-fly oil, the fly is designed to float upon the water. No dry-fly fisherman expects to catch fish. Rather, it is a game of skill in which the score is tabulated by points, as in cribbage. A long, smooth cast, with the fly fluttering lightly down, counts one point. A good float, in which the fly comes dancing lightly downstream on its tiptoes, is good for two points. A rise, that rare occurrence in which a fish comes up, looks at the spurious offering, and says "Phooey," counts ten points. Exciting, isn't it?

Next on the social scale is the pseudo—or non-purist—who employs the same technique as the purist, but who, if a particularly pugnacious trout indicates that it would enjoy smashing a hundred dollars' worth of tackle, will induce his fly to sink for a moment, thus bringing it closer to the fish and, on rare occasions, causing the battle to be joined. If apprehended, the culprit will glibly announce that his dry-fly dope is not working right, or that the trout batted the fly under with its tail.

The distinction between the purist and the pseudo purist is necessarily finely drawn. The purist will speak, but refuses to fraternize, maintaining a dignified reserve becoming to his station. The pseudo purist, on the other hand, always radiates good-fellowship. At times he is even condescending, and is always willing to wager a small amount that the purist dunks one occasionally too, when nobody is looking.

About four rungs down the ladder perches the wet-fly fisherman—a confusing phrase, for all fishermen are more or less amphibious. Technically, the wet fly is designed to travel beneath the surface, thus bringing it more clearly into the fish's range of vision. The optimist who invented it thought that fish would believe it to be edible. That his optimism was justified is evidenced by the fact that on rare occasions the device has been known to work.

The wet-fly fisherman is a lone wolf, for he is ostracized by those above him, while he, in turn, will not speak to the worm fisherman, a pariah who has sunk to such depths of degradation that he will offer fish the type of food they prefer and to which they are accustomed. Even from a distance the casual observer can readily distinguish between the two extremes. All fly-fishermen are gaunt and emaciated, whereas worm fishermen are of a more compact type and appear to be healthy and well-fed.

All fishermen are inconsistent in their whims and fancies, but the dry-fly purist is the worst of the lot, for he is consistently inconsistent. Ask one how many flies are really necessary and he will tell you that a dozen patterns, tied on hooks of various sizes, are all he ever uses, yet he packs along thousands of them on every expedition, leaves other thousands at home, and spends every spare moment tying thousands more. He combs the world for fly-tying materials. He snips hair from the polar bear at the North Pole, and pulls feathers from giant penguins in the Antarctic. He is intimately acquainted with every breeder of gamecocks in six adjoining states, and can call by name every White Wyandotte or Buff Orpington rooster within a hundred miles. The sight of a guinea hen or a male peacock in full plumage will drive him raving crazy, and every dog and cat in his neighborhood has the mangy appearance of a poorly clipped poodle.

In his own home only the family Bible is sacred. Anything else that can be bent or twisted or tied has an uncanny way of disappearing completely, for all is grist that comes to his fly-tying mill. A typical act in his perpetual domestic drama goes something like this.

Scene: His den. Object identifiable as a table, center. Unidentifiable objects everywhere else. The floor would indicate that the world's heavyweight championship has been decided here with the

3

contestants using pillows instead of boxing gloves. The door opens and She enters determinedly, carrying a fur coat that has a motheaten appearance along the bottom.

SHE (*holding coat before him*): "What happened to my coat?"

HE. "Huh? Watch out! There goes that bottle of head lacquer. Look, honey, don't swish that thing over the table. Can't you see that—" (*He rests his head on the table and peers upward in order to get a fish's-eye view of the fly he is tying.*) "Happened to it? Oh, you mean your coat."

SHE (*precisely; in words of one syllable*): "Have you cut fur from this coat?"

HE (*straightens feather on fly*): "There! That ought to do it. What did you say? Oh, yes. Your coat. Let's see now. Seems to me I do remember taking a tiny snip off the bottom. Needed a hair body for a Whangdoodle Special. Worked out swell, too." (*He picks up scissors and eyes coat speculatively.*) "Maybe I'd better trim it up for you; intended to do it but couldn't seem to find the time."

(*She tries to speak but emits only strangled, gurgling sounds as the curtain falls.*)

One of the many unsolved mysteries is why a man who will hestitate for weeks over a simple business problem can instantly determine whether or not he should take a thousand-mile fishing trip and, incidentally, always decide in the affirmative. It may be that the yearning piles up in him like fumes from a leaky gas pipe until the spark, in the form of a printed page or a telephone conversation, touches off the explosion. It may be for some other reason, or lack of it, but with everything presumably under control, his wife will return from an afternoon tea to find the house a shambles, with the lord of the manor coming downstairs three

4

steps at a time, dragging an overstuffed duffel bag and assorted gear behind him.

"Where, in heaven's name . . .?" she begins, but he cuts her short.

"Canada," he says. "Bill phoned. Two weeks. G'bye." And he is gone.

Any sane person would naturally suppose it would be just as much fun to not catch fish in one's own country as to not catch them in Canada, but that supposition is erroneous. The distant horizons have an irresistible appeal to all fishermen. Take, for instance, one of New England's most famous lakes. As soon as it freezes solidly it takes on the air of a military encampment. The ice is dotted with hurrying figures. Squadrons advance while other squadrons recede. Ski-mounted, paper-covered shacks, looking for all the world like Sherman tanks, prowl hither and yon in a seemingly formless pattern, but if anyone watches closely enough, and if he knows fishermen, he will see order emerge from the chaos.

There is a town on either side of the long, narrow lake. In these towns fishermen from miles around assemble to sort out their gear, and then the senseless confusion begins. Those on the west side of the lake start across toward the eastern shore, meeting en route all the east-siders who will fish no other place than the western shore. With the unvarying sameness of migrating birds they keep up the practice until some nonconformist, wandering off the beaten path, catches a fish. Instantly the grapevine flashes the word, and no gold strike in history ever caused a greater stampede.

Wheezy old asthmatics, the lame, the halt, and the half blind grab their chisels, their lines, and minnow buckets and make a grand dash to file a claim near the new discovery. The ice buck-les under the accumulated weight. Chisels flash, ice chips fly, toes are amputated, but in a matter of minutes the ice is honey-combed with holes and fifty lines are down. The school of fish, though, has moved down the lake to the area so recently vacated.

For a few days they will feverishly fish the new location, each one doing his part in upholding the morale of the company by occasionally yanking violently on his line and explaining glibly that he "felt just a touch." Then the fever gradually subsides, and another morning finds them all back on the old treadmill. It's a great game.

I / Nova Scotia

Chet

TROUT WERE THE LODESTONE that had drawn me to Nova Scotia. It was my good fortune that some of the province's officials were anxious for me to see what the interior had to offer in the way of big brook trout, and to that end they had arranged for me to cover Tobeatic Park in the company of Chester Gray, the chief warden of that sanctuary.

It's a queer thing, this habit we have of forming mental pictures of people long before we meet them, and it is queerer still that we are always wrong. My mental image of Chester Gray was of a gray-haired individual with a waistline, an officious manner, and absolutely no sense of humor. Instead, Chester proved to be a black-haired young chap of thirty, with a six-foot body of whalebone and tempered steel, and a pair of dancing, fun-loving brown eyes.

I thought he grasped my hand with unwarranted vigor, and I knew why when he said: "I had the idea you weighed about three hundred pounds, and were the sort of chap who would expect to be carried over every rough portage. Brother, we're going to have fun for the next ten days."

Leaving the car and all of Nova Scotia for the family to enjoy, we stowed my pack and fishing equipment in the warden's car, loaded it down with food, and drove partly over and partly through eighteen miles of wood roads to the tip of Lake Rossignol. This lake, the largest in the province, lies mostly in Tobeatic Park, but there is considerable room left, for the boundaries of the reservation encompass sixteen square miles of almost primeval forest, and the converging lines of Yarmouth, Digby, Shelburne, and Queens counties meet within its borders.

At the shore of the lake we transferred our dunnage to the park boat, a sturdy, salt-water 20-footer, with a tremendous breadth of beam that slowed her down to a six-mile-an-hour crawl. However, I understood the reason for the extreme width. Although the water was like glass at this time, I had a faint idea of what it would be like when a gale howled down across its twenty-mile expanse, and later I was privileged to enjoy a first-hand demonstration of the spectacle.

Some years ago the level of the lake was raised for water-power purposes, and in some of the lower areas the whitened skeleton of towering trees still stood. In the tops of some of them we could see the bulky nests of fish hawks that wheeled endlessly and tirelessly back and forth through the cobalt sky, but not until we threaded an inlet where the dead trees crowded close, did I realize what a mecca these decaying giants were to the feathered folks that I had previously thought of as strictly land birds.

All manner of the woodpecker tribe nested there, including the gigantic and tremendously shy pileated, and in the old caverns they had fashioned in other years, purple martins and swallows and starlings found a safe nesting place. No marauding black snake or squirrel could come here to rob their nests of eggs or young, although I wondered then, and still wonder, just how the newly feathered little fellows managed in their first solo flight. It takes a bit of nerve to crank up and hop off when the nearest land is a quarter mile away.

The lazy May day was drawing to its close when we docked the boat in her slip on the opposite shore. We shouldered our dunnage and struck off upon the mile trail that led to the warden's base camp, which was not a camp at all, but rather a homelike, sturdy affair of peeled logs that sported a substantial paper roof.

I had arrived at last. Nearly 700 miles of gravel and macadam roads lay behind me, and other scores of miles of lakes and rivers and tumbling, bawling trout streams lay before.

It was about time to exchange the paddle for my fly rod and to see what could be dredged up for supper.

Food Packs

MANY A WEARY TRAIL and many a packstrap-galled shoulder has taught me the wisdom of selecting my camping equipment with care and considering first the weight of the food rather than its palatability, but on this occasion I erred.

The fault, though, was not wholly mine. Chet, anxious for my comfort and doubly anxious that every moment of the trip should be wholly pleasing, put me through a rigorous cross-examination concerning the things I liked best to see spread upon the table. When he asked if I cared for tomatoes, I admitted that I was very fond of tomatoes. He discussed canned peaches and peas and all manner of tempting preserves, and I professed my love for them all. The result was that instead of stuffing a small pack with flour and bacon and a few dried fruits and living off the land as I like to do, he crammed all manner of tinned stuff into a big Woods pack, and when the straps were buckled at last, it looked like a small upright piano and weighed scarcely less.

Then there were the sleeping bags. Mine was a lightweight affair, but his was designed for nights when the temperature drops to the zero mark, and it weighed half as much again as mine. There was a small tent that Chet thought it essential to take, for the month was late May, and a two or three days' rain was not at all uncommon at that season. The tent was a thin, oiled affair, designed merely to shed water, but it weighed more than the sleeping bags. I had my personal pack that contained the fewest essential toilet aids but was crammed to the last available inch with all manner of fishing tackle and several hundred flies that I hoped to offer to an equal number of trout.

I have yet to meet the fisherman whose mind does not function along such lines as mine. Personal comfort is a matter of only secondary importance. He will estimate the weight of a skeleton razor and toss it aside without a single qualm, and substitute in its place an extra fly line for which he knows he will have no possible use. A toothbrush, a small cake of soap that will slip from his fingers and go whirling to oblivion down through the rapids the first time he uses it, a towel, and bottle of mosquito dope are the only comforts one usually finds in a fisherman's pack. The rest of the space is given over to things pertaining largely to fish.

It required careful planning to pack my bag, for in addition to the absolutely essential unessentials, I had to find room for all kinds of photographic film and camera supplies. Fish were important, but because they could not be brought home for proof, it was equally important that they be photographed and photographed well. That necessitated, in addition to film and filters and exposure meters and rangefinders, a tried and proven portrait attachment also. I have used one for years and it has been worth far more than its weight in gold to me. I can pose a three-pound brook trout so that the casual observer will estimate its weight as more than double that amount. It is a canny trick and has distinct advantages. I no longer find it necessary to exaggerate about the size of a fish. In fact, when a bulging-eyed acquaintance exclaims as he looks at one of my photographic masterpieces, "Good Heavens! That trout must have weighed seven or eight pounds!" I can assume a modest air and say, "Oh, hardly that. Not more than six, anyway."

We assembled our equipment and, experimentally, Chet draped it upon me piece by piece. He lifted the food pack to my shoulders and adjusted the tumpline across my forehead. He hung the rolled tent and sleeping bags over my right shoulder and hung my camera around my neck. He pooled the straps of his personal pack and mine together, and suspended them from my left shoulder. He stuck the camp ax in my belt, and my knees began to quiver. He added the aluminum dishes, and black spots danced before my eyes. He looped the elastic cord of the landing net over the frypan handle, and everything began to grow dark. Then he handed me my fly rod. It weighed only four ounces but I knew then how the camel must have felt when they added the last straw. I took one faltering step and went down in a heap.

Chet unwound me, piece by piece, and while I lay there gasping, I saw him glance surreptitiously around, then grope in the food pack, extract a can of tomatoes, and toss it into the bush.

"What's the big idea?" I asked. "I thought you were a tomato fiend."

He laughed heartily. "I thought you were," he said. "Personally, I hate the damn things. Let's reorganize that food pack on a commonsense basis."

We went about it at once, discarding most of the canned goods, and when we were finished the big pack weighed no more than I could comfortably swing.

"Okay, Big Boy," I said, "let's go."

Indian Falls

THE SHELBURNE RIVER empties into Lake Rossignol, and its last few miles are fast water. The warden's base camp is located on the upper reaches of that two-mile stretch, with less than an eighth of a mile intervening between it and the quieter waters above. Now where a lot of portaging lies ahead on a trip, the true riverman of the north country, traveling a circuitous and treacherous water route over heartbreaking carries where every excess pound is a handicap, invariably chooses what is known as a guide's canoe. A trifle shorter, a trifle narrower, an extra shaving off each rib and bit of planking, and the end result is that the whole will weigh less than seventy pounds. Chet, knowing me not at all, and choosing like Frank Buck to "bring 'em back alive," elected to use a standard pattern, an eighteen-footer with a slightly greater width of beam, but of ten pounds extra weight. Ten pounds can be quite a lot of trouble under some circumstances—a two-mile carry, for instance, or a shorter distance over a burn or blowdown—but Chet weighed it against the added margin of safety it gave us, and voted for the larger craft.

With the duffel packed neatly amidship, and with me crouching low in the bow, Chet picked up the ten-foot spruce pole, stepped in, and shoved out into the white water. If anyone thinks it is not a clever trick to pole a canoe up through a stretch of swift but shallow water, let him try it sometime. I pride myself on my stamina with a paddle. Nature, plus a certain amount of exercise, has given me wrists and shoulders that can wield a paddle from daylight to dark without suffering swollen muscles or strained tendons, but I have never yet mastered the art of poling. It requires poise and balance, a delicate sense of timing, and long, long practice, and Chet had all of these. We went up through the fast water surely, steadily, and safely, and when at its head he exchanged the pole for his paddle I picked up mine likewise. There was a pleasurable thrill in the bite of the broad blade against the water in that first shoulder surge. Ten days and a hundred or more miles of lakes and streams and rivers and arduous carries lay before us—and civilization lay behind. For a few days it was to be man against the wilderness, and something of the magnitude of the adventure was borne home to me at that moment. Until we had completed the great circle and had dropped down the Roseway into Rossignol once more, we would be compelled to match our forces against those of an untamed and primeval land, and if misadventure came to Chet, as it sometimes does come to even the most skilled woodsman, then it would be I alone.

I think that this is the finest thing about wilderness travel. Civilization robs us of too many God-given essentials that go to make a man, but in the great woods, with the door closed upon the things that lay behind, one reverts to first principles and says to nature, "Array your forces! Bring on your tumbling cataracts and your whitecapped lakes. Bring on your killing portages, the lightning, and the storm, and I'll show you that man, city-weakened though he may be, is yet their master." It does something to a man that is good for his soul.

We drove steadily up through the river until we came to Sand Lake. A cow moose grazed along the shore, thrusting its head far beneath the surface for the bulbous roots of the water lily, but it splashed ashore and disappeared before we came within camera range.

At Indian Falls, at the upper end of Sand Lake, I took my first trout. A tumbling, brawling stream enters the lake here, and at its mouth, in the whitewater rips, the redspots were feeding. We drove the canoe ashore, and wading out to a broad rock that reared itself above the rushing water I laid a streamer fly well out in the rips.

"Socko!"

One says that instinctively when a Nova Scotia trout takes a fly, for they take it as though it were about to be wrested from them. Standing there on that table of rock I took fourteen trout, and all were more than a foot in length. In New Hampshire one would rush home to put them on display in the drugstore window, but up there I released them one by one, changed flies, then laid the line farther out for the big one I knew must be lurking there.

"Double socko!"

He hit it so hard that my light fly rod was bent like a drawn bow, then out into the lake he went, while the reel set up its siren song and the taut line hummed a bewitching accompaniment. For ten minutes it was give and take, with me doing most of the giving and he doing most of the taking, but there came a time when he obeyed the command of the rod and I started the delicate operation of coaxing him up through the white water toward me. I had him up where I could see him, a fine-bodied trout, and Chet was reaching for him with the net when he made a last desperate effort to escape and I applied the pressure too suddenly.

There is no sound so heartbreaking as the faint snap of a parting leader. I reeled in sadly, half inclined to cry, and then I saw that Chet was laughing at me. What sacrilege to laugh at such disaster. I didn't share the knowledge he possessed. I didn't know that hundreds of more glorious pools lay before me.

Beavers

IN DEALING with wildlife, it has been the custom of the American people to take both ends and the middle and give nothing in return, and not until recently have we discovered the error of such a procedure. Promiscuously, and with no thought of the ultimate consequences, we have interrupted the balance of nature. We have stripped our forests and tilled our plains. We have drained our swamps and marshes and made them into arable land that we did not need. We not only took prodigious toll of our wildlife but we robbed it of its home as well, and, worst of all, we set a price upon the head of our beavers and made them a medium of exchange.

No man is qualified to estimate the damage we did to ourselves when we drove into the last remote frontiers those industrious carpenters of the woods. It is an axiom of the northland that whenever beaver are scarce there is also a dearth of other game, and the reverse is equally true. If left to themselves, beaver will transform a wilderness into a game paradise. Their dams store up the surplus water and release it gradually rather than in devastating floods, and water promotes the growth of nearly every living thing. Yes, we erred sadly when we removed the beaver from the scheme of things that nature had planned.

I had gained a speaking acquaintance with them in Maine and in Quebec, but in Tobeatic Park in Nova Scotia I found them at their best, for here they lived in what must have closely approached their original numbers.

Many people more gifted than I are prone to assert that no animal is possessed with reasoning power, but rather is actuated solely by instinct. With them I most joyously disagree, and were I to select an animal with which to refute their argument and prove my own, I think I would choose the beaver.

In the northland, whenever ice closes the streams, the beaver knows that he must store food against the long winter months. It involves a tremendous amount of rush work in the fall to drag in the edible branches and anchor them on the bottom within easy distance of the house. In Tobeatic the labor would be unavailing and the work impossible because many of the more desirable spots—from a homemaking beaver's point of view—are separated from the forests by hundreds of feet of intervening bog and morass.

Under such circumstances, if the beaver were bereft of the power of reason, he would be definitely and decidedly licked, but

24

observation has taught him that some places freeze but thinly if at all. Close to these he builds his house, and from it he travels to the mainland whenever hunger urges him. Whenever the mercury drops to the danger point and the ice begins to close the last bit of open water, he and his family go out and keep it clear by the motion of their bodies, working in relays until the cold snap has passed, then they waddle off through the snow for a repast of maple or poplar twigs, or one of pungent and juicy black birch.

Whenever we camped in the vicinity of a beaver colony, they always came up to look us over just as dusk was falling. I gained the impression that they would have liked to be friendly but had not forgotten the treachery of mankind. Many a night when I had rolled in my sleeping bag and the deadening influence of sleep was creeping over me, I have been aroused by the echoing slap of a broad tail upon the water as the first scout signaled caution to his followers. On one particularly brilliant moonlit night, I sat erect for an hour or more to watch their inquisitive prying into our affairs.

The canoe, upturned upon the bank, drew their attention first. With many a cautious approach and many a faint-hearted retreat, the lone scout viewed it from every possible angle before he crawled out upon the bank beside it. He circled it warily then, at what he judged to be a safe distance, and then when reason told him that it was inanimate and therefore harmless, he went boldly in to verify his judgment.

What signal he made then I do not know, for it was inaudible to my ear, but presently three more of his kind emerged from the water and circled the canoe in turn. Not until then did they notice the white tent beneath the trees, and as one unit they beat a hasty and undignified retreat. They came back, though, swim-

ming cautiously upstream with only the tips of their noses showing, and repeated the maneuver endlessly until I tired of the
waiting and lay down beside the peacefully slumbering Chet.

The beaver builds his house for comfort and serviceability
rather than for ornamental effect. Near a lake entrance, or wherever the rise and fall of the water may be controlled by his dam,
he erects a structure that rises but a few feet above the surface;
however, where strength and height are required to withstand a
ravishing spring freshet, he works from another set of blueprints.

I saw such an example on the Shelburne. How deeply the beaver had been obliged to go to anchor on bedrock I do not know,
but rising above the surface to a height of a few feet beyond the
high-water mark upon the bank, more than ten cords of cut logs
and weathered branches were securely interwoven. From it a
connecting brace extended shoreward, where it was mortared to
a sturdy maple, while from its outer edge a curving ten-foot
wing dam ran upstream to divert the force of any hurrying flood.

It requires some ingenuity to carry a dry log down to the bottom of a stream and leave it there while one goes back for more,
but the beaver knows the answer to that engineering problem.
He knows, too, the value of insulating against summer heat and
winter cold, and achieves that result with successive layers of
wood and sticky mud. He knows how to construct a level floor in
the space reserved for his sleeping quarters, and he knows how to
measure so that the chamber will be just above the high-water
mark. He has learned that in an emergency a pair of backstairs is
worth far more than the labor their construction costs. He knows
everything essential to his self-preservation—with one exception.
He has not yet learned to successfully cope with avaricious, ruth-
less, and shortsighted mankind. I hope that some night as he lies

26

securely within his cozy retreat and listens to the Arctic wind that howls and shrieks in baffled fury above him, he may reason out the answer to that problem also.

Sand Lake

To CATCH TROUT in New England one would have to go back about fifty years. To catch them in Nova Scotia one need not go back more than fifty miles.

I do not mean to say that there are no more big trout in New England waters. Probably, if the truth were known, many an old sockdolager lies in his sheltered retreat under the submerged log that has sheltered many others of his kind, but you can't prove it by me. I have taken some that might truthfully be called big, but they come less frequently than of old, and on those rare occasions when I do land one I have the uneasy feeling that perhaps he is the last of the Mohicans. The squaretail is a wary fellow and if he has once felt the prick of a barbed hook he is more than likely to be careful for a time, but the odds are heavily against him. It may well be that in the course of a single season a hundred fishermen will offer him a thousand different flies, and sooner or later he will make a mistake.

In Nova Scotia, though, barring the natural enemies that prey upon him, a trout's chance of reaching a ripe old age is multiplied a thousandfold.

As yet, man has not entered the picture, or at least only superficially, and millions of trout in the interior have never seen the shimmering shadow of a leader dancing on a sandbar, nor viewed the enticing wriggle of a sunken fly. They are there, an innumerable host, and, like all other healthy living things, are hungry upon occasion.

It is universally believed that if one fishes virgin waters he can take fish wherever and whenever he chooses, but such has not been my experience. Early in the season when the waters are still icily cold, I have found trout taking best during the middle of the day, but as the temperature of the streams rises they feed most heavily at dawn and dusk. Of late, prophets have arisen to proclaim that the appetites of all fish may be accurately charted years in advance, and that the precise moment may be foretold in which a trout as yet unhatched will take a fly; but I am still happily of the older school of thought, and believe such theories to be pure and unadulterated bunk. Fish lead normal lives, as every hatchery superintendent knows. Under normal conditions they assimilate food, digest it, and are hungry again, and the process goes on without change until some upheaval of nature disturbs the routine. A rain that makes the clear waters a coffee-colored flood; a wind that stirs it to devastating fury; sudden cold or intense heat—any of these may cause a fish to forget its hunger in the more absorbing battle for existence. In the wild, where nature has unrestricted sway, such conditions occur with greater frequency and oftentimes with greater violence, but when things return to normal again one needs neither calendar nor tide table in order to catch fish—at least not if he chances to be in the interior of Nova Scotia.

We found good trout in the Shelburne, the first day out from camp. It was a cool day because a drizzling rain was falling, and consequently each pool showed the ripple of feeding trout. It was an interesting day, for I had yet to learn how large a trout must be for Chet to classify it as big. It had been mutually understood before we started out that we would kill no fish other than the ones we needed for the frypan and those other martyrs that the camera lens would immortalize. The farther up the Shelburne we went, the bigger the fish grew, but still Chet carefully netted them, held them up a moment for me to gloat over, then slipped them back into the water. That was all right for the half-pounders, but when we got where I was consistently taking fish of more than a foot in length I began to wonder. Didn't he call a fourteen-inch fish a good one? Back home, if a chap came in with a half dozen like that, he'd see their picture in the paper next day, under some such caption as "Joe Bogardus Takes Record String." And Chet didn't even give them a second look. They might have been crappies or perch for all the interest he displayed. Good enough for pan fish, but hardly worth writing home about.

Then, at the upper end of Sand Lake, I tied into a good fish. A brawling stream entered the lake there, the tumultuous current leaping down to the last rock barrier that barred its path, and beyond it some good trout were feeding.

The logical place to take them was from the lake side, where they could be led out into deep water and fought to a finish, but that sort of thing never appealed strongly to me. With the whole lake in which to fight them, the fisherman had every advantage, and if he took plenty of time he could wear down any trout. When the situation was reversed, however, it was a different matter. Standing on the rocky shore and casting out to the edge of the reef, the trout had something to say concerning the outcome. If he chose to be led up through the rapids to a waiting net it might be necessary for him to pay the penalty for his mistake, but if he chose rather to stay outside and make a fight of it, then it was skill and four ounces of springy bamboo that were pitted against maddened brute strength. We went ashore.

From the last solid boulder on which I could safely stand it was a comfortable cast to the still water beyond the reef. I laid a streamer fly out there, waited a moment for it to submerge, then started a slow retrieve.

"Socko!" In the jargon of a fisherman, the word has its own peculiar place, for no other is so descriptive of the manner in which a heavy and hungry brook trout takes a fly. Alone in a big pool, a fat old trout may rise lazily, but when feeding in company with a half dozen others of his kind he does not hesitate. If he does, the luckless minnow or crawfish goes down another gullet.

Volumes have been written about how to hook a rising trout, but I have yet to see the time when anything but a stiff wrist is necessary if the fish is hungry enough. This one struck like a brick dropped from a tenth story, and the rod took on an arc that never once straightened for the ensuing ten minutes.

All the evidence pointed toward the fact that this was a good fish. When he wanted line he took it, and he took it in great, strong rushes that all the power of the little rod would not check.

The best proof of his size, however, was in Chet's face. I glanced at him once, and for the first time that day he was showing real interest. Standing beside me with the net in his hand, he was leaning forward as though he, too, were fighting the battle, and the knuckles of his hand showed white when he gripped the net.

There's a thrill that is hard to match in the taking of big trout. I imagine it would be a prosaic business to pull them in hand over hand on a cod line, but when one uses a rod of not more than four ounces a man's nerve is better than mine if his pulse doesn't double its beat. The slender wand of bamboo seems wholly inadequate. It bends in a rainbow curve and seems not to retard the frightened fish in the least, but it is relentless in its persistent tension and gradually it wears the warrior down.

The trout fought its battle before the rock barrier and he fought it well, but the time came when he signified that he was done. I saw the white of his belly as he rolled sluggishly, and after that it was only a matter of time before I brought him up through the rapids to the net. Chet scooped him up, held him aloft the better to peer at him, and then all the animation went out of his face.

"Hm-m-ph!" he said. "He fooled me. I thought it was a good trout, but he won't go over two and a half pounds." He turned the net over and let the vanquished warrior slip back into the stream. "Let's get out of here," he said. "This place isn't worth bothering with. There's some better pools up above."

Big Game

WE WERE HALFWAY ACROSS the mile-long portage between House and Junction lakes, and I for one was ready to stop. Every inch of that half mile that lay behind us was an uphill drag, and my knees were beginning to wobble.

There is a spiritual uplift, though, in realizing that one has reached the halfway point. To know that half the backbreaking toil is done, and that one more step will launch a fellow on the short end of the journey, does more to revive tired muscles than anything else I know. It was good, though, to slip off the pack-straps and let the load slide to the ground, and I noted that even Chet, inured to that delightful sort of drudgery though he was,

33

breathed a sigh of relief as he leaned the bow of the canoe high up against a granite boulder and stepped out from under it.

We had topped the height of land, and now the ground sloped easily away from us in all directions; a barren, rock-strewn waste in which only blueberry bushes and stunted hemlocks grew. It was the first day of June and still delightfully cool. The air, sweeping across the treeless expanse, fanned us gently and we opened our shirt fronts gratefully and let it evaporate the moisture from our steaming breasts.

Standing there, gazing off into the west, a distant movement caught my eye: a flash of color that moved from behind a clump of bushes and was gone instantly. Strange it is how a hunter's heart will leap in moments such as this. Even though he be armed only with a camera, his reflexes instinctively follow the course in which they have been trained to move, and every sense is sharpened as the primal forces that are in every man gain ascendancy. I watched for a moment longer, feeling my heartbeat increase its tempo as I did so, then spoke to Chet. "There's game of some sort moving out there," I said.

That Chet was also a hunter was proven by the way in which he moved. He did not start nor turn quickly about. Instead, he merely lifted his eyes interrogatively to mine and asked, "Where?"

"Straight into the wind," I told him. "A half mile away."

He turned slowly, an inch at a time, until he faced the direction I had indicated, and standing there together we watched for long moments. Presently we caught the movement again, and almost instantly thereafter a telltale flash of white that was unmistakable. We were looking at the first of many deer that I was to see on the trip through a land in which that species of game is probably more abundant than anywhere else in eastern North America.

The wind was in our favor, and contrary to its usual custom the deer was traveling with it. Its course, erratic though it was, would eventually bring it somewhere near the spot where we stood. Slowly, unobtrusively, I sank down upon the ground, crawled over to the duffel pile, and dug out my camera.

There is, I think, no animal more graceful in its movements than the white-tailed deer. The hunter, his trigger finger itching while he watches with covetous eyes, is blinded to the things the nature lover is quick to see, and I regret that it took me so many years to learn this fact. How infinitely more satisfying to crouch there behind the rock, just peeping over the top of it, with our hats pulled low to shadow the betraying white of our faces, and watch the dainty creature make its way toward us. Totally unaware of our presence, it had none of the furtive movement so characteristic of its kind in heavily hunted areas. It came on fearlessly, pausing ever and anon to lower its head and nibble at some tender shoot in its path, then breaking into a brisk trot for a few steps as though to compensate for the moments it had wasted. On several different occasions when a boulder barred its path, it leaped cleanly over it, and those bounds were the very essence of poetry. There was no settling back for the spring, as in the cat family, but without so much as an instant's halt in its stride, and with no perceptible tightening of its muscles, it would fold its forelegs beneath its body and rise up and up to soar like a bird cleanly over the obstruction.

On it came and now it was evident that it would pass below the crest of the hill a hundred or more yards to our left. I had not noticed before, but now I saw that an old moose path lay there, and it was this the deer was following. If I were to get pictures of it I must act at once. I waited until a clump of spruces separated us, then scrambled up and dashed for a protecting bit of cover somewhat nearer the trail. Twice more I did it and was within thirty feet of the well-worn path when the deer, that now was less than fifty yards away, stopped instantly, with all four feet braced. It had not seen me, of that I was certain, but some errant flaw of wind had wafted the dreaded man-scent in its direction. As though washed from it with a giant sponge, all the careless and easy grace was gone from the creature in a moment. It was a hunted thing, frozen into rigid immobility because of that hated man taint that it could not for the moment locate. Then, so swiftly that it appeared to turn a back somersault, it wheeled about and set off across country at a speed that but few four-footed things can equal, while I watched it with interest and no little chagrin. I realized that I was dust-grimed and sweaty, but it was hardly complimentary to think that even the sensitive nose of a deer could catch the reek of my body from a distance of fifty yards downwind.

We saw four deer that day and seven the next. After that, it was a common sight, when we rounded a bend, to see one or more standing at the water's edge, with head upraised and star-tled eyes staring at the strange creature that floated so noiselessly toward it.

Although every portage we trod was nothing more than a well-worn moose path, every one of them was bisected at dozens of places by other paths that crossed at diverging angles. In addi-tion to numerous bear signs along the trails, it was not unusual for us to distinguish among them the rounded imprint of the pad of a Canada lynx, a greater enemy by far to the deer tribe than is the killer, man.

Ducks thundered up from the streams before us, and I do not recall seeing a lake that did not shelter at least one flock. Mother ducks hugged the shores of the rivers and called frantically to their straying broods as we swept past. On one occasion we stumbled upon such a family on one of the carries, and shed canoe and packs hastily that we might give chase not to the crafty mother, who went limping and fluttering through the bush before us, but to the downy little chaps that scattered in all directions and went swiftly and silently away. We caught two of them after a hard chase, and held them in our hands for a moment while we stroked their soft, warm down and vowed our intentions were honorable. But the hammering of their little hearts against our fingers was so pitiful that we set them down shortly, and watched them scurry away toward the mother, who was calling frantically from the bush.

The only thing lacking on that enchanted land was the thunder of rising grouse. For some reason, that grandest of all upland game birds does not thrive in Nova Scotia. There are and always will be a few of them, but I doubt if they ever approach the numbers found in a similar area in northern New England in the years when the cycle of production is at its peak. By way of compensation, the province furnishes the finest woodcock shooting in all the world. Breeding extensively throughout its length and breadth, they work southward at the beginning of the fall migration, to concentrate at last in Yarmouth country, and it is to Yarmouth country that I am going some day ere long. Chet has promised to meet me there, that we may be together for a week. It may not be this year, for with such turmoil as the world is in at the present moment, the future is largely a matter of conjecture. But I'm going to give it a try, brother, I'm going to give it a try.

Portaging

THE FIRST TWO DAYS that we were in Tobeatic Park there was ample evidence that man had preceded us. For several miles up the Shelburne we were continually forced to dodge pulpwood bolts that came floating down from distant cuttings, but as we neared Irving Lake we began to leave these evidences of civilization behind us. It happens that I am one of those misguided chaps to whom the far horizons always seem the fairest, and I like best to tread those forest trails where one does not bump into a camping party of Girl Scouts at every turn. Not that I am averse to company. I've spent many a pleasant day on waterways that were crowded, but when I do choose to absorb a bit of nature in the raw I like to feel that I am so far removed from the customary haunts of men that it will take something more than a lusty shout of mine to bring a half dozen of them running from as many different directions.

It required a hard day's toil from the warden's base camp to induce that feeling within me, but as we reached our objective and the night began to close in around us I could feel the solitude creeping in also. We were getting in back of beyond. We had driven eighteen miles over the paper company's road to Lake Rossignol, and had added another eleven miles to the distance by cutting across one end of that formidable body of water. Then we had hiked a mile into camp. That meant we were about thirty miles in the woods. Poling through stretches of rapids and carrying around the places where poling was impossible, together with the waiting while I fished some of the most enticing pools, had cut our mileage down on the second day but when we set the canoe down in Irving Lake forty miles of winding trail lay behind us. Quite definitely—and quite pleasingly—we were getting into the woods, but as yet we were not far enough to suit me. Each portage over which we had carried and each lake that we had crossed were still sharply etched in my mind, and I knew that if occasion demanded it I could find my way back alone, without the aid of either map or compass. But the time was coming when I would not feel so confident, for the end of the third day out found me delightfully lost. True, I had my diary, a clearly understandable map and a thoroughly reliable compass, and I like to think that I could have made some sort of port by their aid, but not by memory alone. We had crossed too many lakes and carried our duffel over too many winding forest trails for my brain to remember them all.

It was then, when I realized that if Chet were suddenly eliminated from the scene I would be dependant upon those things that I had learned about woodcraft to get me safely out, that the trip began to take on the glamour that attends true wilderness travel.

Unconsciously, and out of the confusion that came from trying to remember too much, my mind took on a new sharpness. A wooded point that jutted out into a lake, a V-shaped block of granite standing upright at a river bend, a half-obliterated scar upon the trunk of a stunted maple that marked the beginning of a portage. It was these inanimate things, the signboards that pointed the way back over the trail we had come, that engraved themselves upon my memory, and so sharply etched were they that I would have recognized the originals had I met them in Europe. I can still see them as clearly as though I had viewed them within the hour.

There was a spiritual exultation beyond comparison in that great isolation, and the feeling became intensified on the long carries that continually confronted us. As I have explained, our technique after a few experimental tries became a routine affair. When it was necessary to haul out, Chet would steer up to some poorly defined game trail that led down to the water, and as he held the canoe steady I would step out and draw it well up on the bank. When he had clambered up beside me, we would unload our entire cargo, and I would struggle into the rib-saving pack composed of the tent and our sleeping bags. On top of that bulky load Chet would swing the food pack and adjust the tumpline across my forehead. Then he would hoist the overturned canoe upon his capable shoulders and strike off, leaving me to puff and pant along behind him.

40

The one drawback to this procedure was the fact that his personal pack and mine, my camera, fly rod and landing net, the dishes, cooking utensils, and camp ax had to be left behind. That necessitated a return trip. At first we went back together and shared the load, but it was wasted energy to compel two men to do one man's work, and the wilderness teaches conservatism in the matter of strength. Therefore we abandoned the practice in favor of the simpler plan of alternating on the return trips, and letting one go back after the remaining duffel while the other rested.

I liked those return trips alone, despite the toil that attended them. The trails were always poorly defined. They had been spotted years before (an ax blaze on a tree to mark a change of course, for example), but the years had almost obliterated the marks and it required an experienced eye to pick them up readily. When the portage lay along an unnavigable stretch of a stream, one had the comforting assurance that if he lost the trail he could always make his way over to the water and follow it down to the quieter reaches below where the canoe would be waiting; but when the way led across country from one lake to another, one's mental reaction was quite likely to be entirely different. It is a stimulating sensation to wonder just how far it will be necessary to walk if a fellow misses the lake that lies somewhere ahead.

Another never-failing source of interest was the fact that each of the portages lay through what is undoubtedly the most prolific game territory in eastern North America. Many of the trails we trod were deeply worn moose paths, and we saw the awkward, shambling creatures on several different occasions. Many a time, while toiling along with my back bowed beneath its load and my eyes fixed on the trail at my feet, I have stepped into the fresh imprint of a bear's track so large that my own moccasined foot would not overlap its length. I know from personal experience gained in many days hunting for them that bears are the shiest of all the woods dwellers, but nevertheless there was always a pleasurable thrill in realizing that at that moment a four-hundred-pounder might be testing the air for my scent from a distance of less than a stone's throw. Under such circumstances, even though he is not afraid, one unconsciously raises his eyes to view the nearest tree, and to note with satisfaction that the lower limbs are within easy reach.

Chet told me that on one occasion while carrying across a portage alone, he came upon the body of a freshly killed doe that lay directly across the trail. He was within a few hundred feet of the lake at the time, therefore he went on, set the canoe down on the shore and went back to investigate. The doe was gone, and in the soft earth where she had lain were mammoth bear tracks. The big fellow had lifted her bodily and borne her away.

"Did you find her?" I asked.

"Not me," he answered. "It was his dinner not mine. I didn't feel that it was my place to go in and take it away from him."

The Sesketch

IF YOU WERE to conduct a poll on either Nova Scotia or Quebec in order to determine which one of a hundred standard patterns of trout flies was the most popular, I'd venture to say that a Dark Montreal would lead the list. In both these places it seems to be the custom to twine several of this variety in one's hatband. For a reason not known to me the flies are looked upon as something that every well-dressed fisherman should wear, and seemingly imply that at least concerning all things piscatorial, the wearer knows his way around.

As accurately as I can recall, I have never yet taken a worthwhile trout on a fly of that pattern. I keep a few in my fly books to be used in self-defense whenever it is necessary, and on several different occasions when a dusky-skinned Montagnais guide has insisted on it, I have tied one on and made a few desultory casts with it, but as far as I am concerned it still remains a dud.

In Caledonia, where we outfitted, Chet pored over my fly book before we started out. Perhaps, if you insist upon accuracy, it would be better if I used the plural, for there were several books, and I prided myself that they were all well stocked. There were scores of patterns in various sizes of wets and dries, bass bugs and fuzzy bivisibles, wiggly nymphs, and two immense aluminum boxes into the cork lining of which I had impaled row after row of streamers that were a very kaleidoscope of color. Chet looked them over and shook his head in disappointment. "I can see only three Montreals," he said. "You ought to have more. It's a great fly up here."

I told him that I was aware of it, and that I had intended to pick up a dozen in Liverpool but it had slipped my mind. I suggested that when these three were worn to a frazzle it was still remotely possible that we might induce at least a few trout to try something else for a change. He didn't believe it, for he went through his personal belongings and dug out four additional ones in various stages of dissolution, to be used as a sort of reserve fund to save us from bankruptcy, and then we started out.

We carried four portages that day, and my fishing was consequently restricted, yet using a light Edson Tiger (a three-inch yellow bucktail) I took twenty-three trout, many of which were more than a foot in length, while two would have gone more than a pound in weight.

There wasn't much that Chet could say except that the trout seemed to like the fly, so to vindicate my belief that big fish were not averse to big lures, I tied on a green-and-white Supervisor on the morning of the second day. It was a larger creation than the first, but we were getting back into the land of big trout, and the way they smashed that oversize monstrosity was something to remember.

We reached the Sesketch on the evening of the third day, and on the morning of the fourth our fun really began. It was Chet's job to patrol the park and see that no misfortune befell the wildlife in his charge. Consequently it was also his job to check the men who invaded any part of his domain during the fishing season.

That night as we lay in our sleeping bags and listened to the waters of the Sesketch tumbling down into a pool below our camp, he said, "We ought to pick up some good fish tomorrow. We're getting back now where it isn't fished much. A couple of fellows came through here last year, traveling light, but nobody's been here this year, and probably won't be now, for it's getting late in the season."

All at once I realized that this was the mecca for which I had been searching so long. At last we were back of beyond, on as good a trout stream as lies anywhere on the eastern seaboard, and I would be the first man to drop a fly in it in the last two years. I shivered in anticipation.

The day had been a hard one. We had traveled from crack of dawn to deep dusk, and I was as tired as a man has a right to be after carrying and paddling and fishing for fourteen hours, but all at once I found myself wishing that it was morning. I slept fitfully, and awakened a dozen times to see if it was growing light in the east.

Chet was something more than a guide, at least he differed from some guides I have known, for without so much as a hint

from me he was boiling coffee at three thirty the next morning.
He-man's coffee. Coffee with a lot of zip and tang to it. The sort
of coffee that sets a fellow up on his toes and makes him peer
around for a wildcat or two to lick. It was an appropriate frame
of mind in which to be, for in another half hour the battle of the
century would begin.

There was no doubt in my mind when I saw the place that this
was the spot I had been searching for for years. Through countless centuries of floods and freshets the stream had worn its way
down through the granite to form a giant staircase whose sides
were straight and deeply cut. Down this gorge the water cas-
caded in a white rage at being restrained in its headlong plunge
to reach the circular pool at its base.

The pool itself was perhaps a hundred feet across, and deep
and dark and mysterious. Every pool like that has its own favored
spot to which the Lord Mayor of the pool claims ownership, and
it was my job to drift a fly down on it. Carefully, with Chet following close behind me, I worked up from jutting handhold to
jutting handhold along the face of the gorge until I was halfway
up the flume. Out there in midstream a giant boulder reared its
head, and the water just below it showed green. That meant
depth, and depth meant that this surely must be the place where
the old man lived. I flicked the streamer out into the flood and let
it drift down past the boulder.

Here and there in one place or another I have been mistaken
in thinking that a small trout was a large one, but I have never
hooked a really good fish without knowing it for what it was. It
was so in this case. There was a feeling of power that tele-
graphed along the line to me that no small fish could equal.

"Big trout," I said, but Chet shook his head.

"Just fair," he said, and in that moment the fish leaped clear of the water and shook himself like a water-soaked dog. The trout, to my startled gaze, looked to be at least three feet long.

"Well, maybe a little better than fair," Chet said.

The trout, so long the monarch of the pool, didn't like the restraint and went circling around and around only to make a dash for the white water and go boring upstream with a power I could not stay. Then it leaped the low waterfall at the head of the flume and went tearing up through the stream beyond my sight or hearing. I am not sure that it is true, but it very well could be that I am the only man in the world who has played a redspot trout in water that was higher than his head, but play him I did, keeping a reasonably tight line, and after a fight that seemed to have taken hours, I managed to steer him up through the white water to Chet's waiting net.

It was a beautiful fish, unusually deep, and colored by a pink flush that would be blood-red when October and the spawning season came around again. Its weight, the scale declared, was three pounds and six ounces. No matter where he may live, no angler need feel shame when he hooks his fingers into the gills of a brook trout of that size, and no man need be ashamed of a trout chowder such as Chet threw together back at camp. When we had licked the dishes clean we were ready to tackle the problems of another day. But not such a long one, I hoped. Chet's watch said that it was not yet six o'clock.

Forest Music

THE GOVERNMENTS of Nova Scotia and Quebec err, I think, in granting concessions to lumber companies to operate within the limits of their park reservations. That there are strict regulations concerning the number of trees they may take, I will admit, but it is my belief that not one should be cut.

To my mind, at least, the aesthetic qualities of a wilderness are seldom improved when man takes a hand in its beautification. Too often he goes through a piece of woodland and sweeps and dusts and polishes, leaving it as spick-and-span as a city park but not at all like nature in the raw.

The lumberman in Nova Scotia are less housewifely. They

ply their axes industriously and let the chips and branches fall where they may. The result is that along the outer fringes of Tobeatic there are miles of slashings that form a very definite fire hazard. I believe that it is a shortsighted policy that sets aside a tract of land for game conservation and then permits the animals to be menaced by a thing that some day will inevitably develop into a roaring inferno that no human hand can stay.

Fortunately, not only for wildlife but for men and women who love nature as God made it, there are several tracts within the park that will never echo the blows of a woodsman's ax. Numberless lakes and ponds dot the flat expanse and these are connected by shallow, winding streams. It is the latter that affords an effective check to the lumberman's greed. As a rule, they are too narrow and too shallow to float heavy logs efficiently. Such stuff may be rafted and towed laboriously across lakes, or run swiftly and easily in the rivers, but not with any marked degree of success in streams along which a canoe must be threaded carefully among countless upthrust boulders, or steered around abrupt, right-angle bends.

Fortunately, too, from my viewpoint, many of the streams are separated from the mainland by several hundred feet of muskegs that do not freeze solidly in winter. This eliminates the use of horses and the more efficient tractor, and assures the wildlife, in the interior at least, a sanctuary that will still be unchanged a hundred years hence.

It was worth any price to me to be able to fish in a country so virgin. And it was worth almost as much to tread the dim aisles of forests that had never known the defiling hand of man. For the first three days our course lay through granite country: hard, unyielding, stubborn country eminently suited to a lumberman's need and equally unsuited to the delicate covering of a canoe. The beds of the streams were floored with granite and every jutting fragment possessed a razor edge. It was the bowman's place to locate each subsurface rock and swerve the canoe so as to avoid disastrous contact with it; but in dodging one I oftentimes hit two more, and the result was that we were obliged to haul out several times and apply patches of pitch to numerous clean incisions in the fabric.

The labor ended abruptly when we left the granite country, for the rocks no longer had power to harm. The land grew flatter, the streams wider and more sluggish, the lakes more frequent, while the timber grew as nature intended timber should grow—in rugged and primal grandeur.

We left our regular route, at my insistence, and went several miles out of our way just to see a growth of virgin white pine. Virgin pine is a thing upon which few present-day Americans have looked, for it went the way of the buffalo and the passenger pigeon, and it went, I fear, never to return. I hesitate to use a word made noxious by Hollywood, but "colossal" is the only adequate term to describe the trees, which were immense, gigantic. Chet's arm spread coupled with mine totaled nearly twelve feet, but even together we could encircle only the boles of the smaller trees. Multitudes of them, towering majestically aloft, were far larger. They had been old, as we count age, when the province was young, and they would be standing there, sturdy and strong, when we had gone over our last portage. I utter no idle prophecy for they rest secure in their remote fastness. Two small fortunes have been sunk in trying to bridge the blessed spans of muskegs that guard them from the invaders, and still they stand there, defying time and the fierce winds that sweep across from Fundy.

I shall go back to Nova Scotia some day—I hope—for I want to lay a fly in the Sesketch again, and I particularly desire to walk among those majestic giants once more.

Longfellow sang of "the murmuring pines and the hemlocks." I agreed with him so far as pines were concerned, but I considered his use of hemlocks a rather flagrant example of poetic license, yet one day I learned that he was right and that it was I who erred.

We were carrying from one lake to another, and Chet had gone ahead with the canoe. Bowed with the weight of my load, I was struggling along some distance in the rear, when I suddenly heard a great organ playing. The sound came from somewhere before me and I went on eagerly, for organ music has a strange power to stir my soul. Presently I found myself in a great cathedral. Towering hemlock trunks rose all around me, stretching upward for fifty—sixty—seventy feet to where the lofty and interwoven branches barred the sunlight. Among these branches the wild winds stirred, and the effect was one of celestial music. Soft, resonant, deep, it sang of a time when God walked in the cool of the forest. Then as the wind played upon muted pipes, the chorus rose, full, swelling, triumphant, a mighty diapason of sound that held me breathless.

I slipped off my pack and, unmindful of time and place, sank down upon it to revel in that glorious harmony. I might have been sitting there yet, spellbound beyond all power of movement, had Chet not grown worried when I failed to arrive at the lake. He came back and found me, but when he tried to hurry me away, I demurred. I drew him down beside me, and with the day's journey only half done and with many a weary hike lying before us, we sat there together and listened.

53

Divided Trail

I LIKE BEST to travel trails alone. It is a more profitable sort of venture, for one sees ever so many more things when he can set his own pace and depend on his own eyes rather than those of his guide. I remember that one carry on the West Branch was especially interesting and, in addition, gave Chet a few anxious minutes.

The portage was a long one, and because the course lay downstream, Chet, as he often did, suggested that it would be advisable for him to take the canoe down through the rapids alone while I negotiated the trail that led to the quiet waters below. He was not shirking his duty, for he was a glutton for work. It really

54

made the carry easier for me, for in order to trim the canoe properly for stability and ease of handling in the white water, he needed something like seventy-five pounds of good, solid dunnage to pack into it, just forward of amidships, to balance his weight in the stern.

Nothing in our outfit was so admirably suited to that purpose as our thrice-accursed food pack, for it possessed weight without bulk and could be wedged solidly under the forward thwart where no sudden tilt could dislodge it and overbalance the frail craft at a moment when perfect balance was essential if disaster were to be averted.

We followed the plan on numerous occasions, and we did so for two reasons. The first was that Chet's chief concern at all times was for my safety and comfort, and not once would he take a chance that involved any risk while I was in the canoe. Later, when our teamwork had improved and as we had grown to know each other better, I think he would have risked shooting some of the less turbulent rapids with me aboard had not the second factor entered the scheme of things.

I was a guest of the government, and it was only natural to suppose that they hoped for some tangible returns through the advertising my fishing stories would give them. Pictures, then, became an absolute necessity. The officials recognized their advertising value, but I had a more intimate knowledge of their worth, for a half dozen good photographs have sold many a poor story of mine. Unflatteringly, as day followed day and the pile of exposed negatives grew hourly larger within their waterproof bag, they became the things of first importance and usurped the position that I had formerly enjoyed. Chet understood this, and while I like to think that he learned to have some confidence in me and came to believe that I was as capable of taking care of myself as was he if the canoe went out from under us, he knew that if the camera and film were lost it would be disaster indeed.

Thus, when on this particular occasion we swung in to the bank and I heard the roar of turbulent water below us, I had no presentiment that anything more than a delightful stroll through the woods awaited me.

"I'll ease her down through," Chet said, and began tossing duffel out on the bank. "It's a long carry—at least a mile—so take your time." He slid the food pack under the thwart and lashed it securely there with a turn of the packstrap. "The trail splits about halfway across. You'll see a big maple, spotted on both sides. You take the left fork."

That reminded me of the old wheeze about the left glove being right while the right one was left, and when I pulled it on Chet he laughed politely, as though he were hearing the gag for the first time. Then he eased the canoe from the bank, stepped in and headed downstream, while I began to lift the packs, one after another, onto my shoulders.

Few fatalities are caused by mountains falling upon people. Rather, it is the little things that often have the most serious consequences, and in this instance it was the landing net that caused all the trouble. The system I had worked out through a trial-and-error method was to slip the camera around my neck so that it hung in front. Then I would slip into the harness that bound the tent and sleeping bags together. Above it I would hoist my personal pack, while upon it, with straps shortened so that it might ride securely upon my left shoulder, I would hoist the nested mess kit and cooking utensils. Lastly, like a prima donna gracing herself with a rope of pearls, I would slip the elastic cord of the landing net over my lead and let the ring drape itself behind me. Then, with my fly rod in one hand and the other left free to brush away the ever-present mosquitoes, I would start out.

The one drawback to this otherwise perfect arrangement was that the meshes of the net had a fiendish way of catching on every substantial bit of brush that swung into the path behind me, while I, bent beneath my load, would plow steadily ahead until the cord, tightening around my throat, warned me of impending disaster. No matter how quickly I paused I was invariably a split second too late, for the twig would seize that moment to break, while the cord that was now stretched to its fullest extent would propel the net handle directly at the back of my defenseless head with all the speed and accuracy of an arrow launched from a yeoman's bow.

It was a good joke, but after a score of repetitions it was only natural that it should lose some of its zest. Therefore on this occasion I looped both net and cord over the protruding frypan handle and felt that I had solved a major problem.

I located the trail without difficulty, a well-worn moose path with spotted saplings at strategic intervals along it. It was a cool day, my load was not excessive, and the mosquitoes were less affectionate than usual. All went well until I reached the fork of the trail, and then because of the inane doggerel I had repeated concerning the left being right while the right one was left, I could not for the life of me remember which branch I was to take.

It was a matter that required some deliberation, so I began shedding my load so that I might sit down and think it over. It was then that I discovered the landing net was gone, snatched off in midair by some demoniac bush along the trail. Next to the films and fly rod it was of the utmost importance, and there was nothing to do but go back after it. Leaving the duffel where it was I went back. I went back and back and back, but not until I was within a hundred feet of our landing place did I find the net, swinging contentedly on the first bush that had crossed our path.

Meanwhile, Chet had run the rapids and was hurrying back to share my load. At the fork of the trail he found my dunnage pile, and since he had not met me on the trail it was self-evident that I had taken the other one. He did not stop to consider that I might have retraced my steps. He had, I think, a shrewd suspicion that all writers were slightly cuckoo, and he knew that the right-hand path led into an almost impenetrable moose bog. He shouted, then hurried down it to rescue me while rescuing was still possible.

All unaware of this, I came back, saddled myself with my load, and determining to find out first where the left trail led, struck out upon it. The canoe was there at the end of it, resting snugly under the bank, but Chet was neither there nor within answering distance of my shout.

I wonder sometimes how he and I could become such fast friends when our temperaments differed so widely. There was he, fretting and fuming because of my idiocy as he hurried down the path to find me, and there was I, neither knowing where he was nor caring particularly, for a perfect trout pool lay just below the last rapid. I shed my packs, donned the landing net (suspended again by the cord around my neck), picked up the fly rod, waded out, and hooked a two-pound trout on the first cast. I was still at it ten minutes later when Chet came back. Despite the coolness of the day, he was perspiring freely, and although he concealed it well, I have no doubt he was more than a little

peeved with me. He had no reason to be, however, for I was entirely without blame. The fault lay with that capricious landing
net.

Moose

I AWAKENED SUDDENLY. It was only half light, but around me was
a deeper blackness. For a moment I lay there listening, while my
mind, numbed by sleep, strove to orient itself. Then I remembered. We were camping at Spectacle Lake. The gray mist that
eddied and swirled before me was the vapor rising from the
warm waters. The shadows behind me, gloomy and somber and
mysterious, were the impenetrable forest. I remembered the
scene then, as it was when we had pitched camp less than eight hours
before. The lake, bifurcated and connected by a crooked isth-
mus, was strongly reminiscent of a pair of nose glasses: hence its
name. Our tiny tent was spread almost at the water's edge, and

there was reason for it. In that land of muskeg and bog, mosquitoes swarm in innumerable hordes that are beyond the conception of one who has not warred against them. Within the forest, sleep would only be possible after one had swathed oneself in fold upon fold of mosquito netting, and even then the high, whining note of the winged hosts as they whirled and circled and probed for an opening in the armor was not conducive to dreamless sleep.

Experience, however, had taught us both that there was a way to circumvent the pests. Usually a night wind stirred across most large bodies of water, and by pitching camp close to shore on that side toward which the breeze moved, one could sleep unencumbered by the mummy-like wrappings.

We had followed that plan the previous evening, but because the night was cloudless I had chosen to spread my sleeping bag outside the tent, with the wavelets that murmured along the gravelly shore to soothe me, and the silent, white stars for company.

As I lay there, I wondered what had awakened me so suddenly. Within the tent, I could hear Chet's regular breathing, and I knew he had not stirred. I listened, but save for the wash of the water at my feet, and the sleepy murmur of the wood, there was no other sound. Then I heard it again—the unmistakable sound of a heavy footfall from somewhere close at hand. Cautiously, silently, I sat erect and looked about. The forest, crowding closely upon the shore, was still forbiddingly dark, but almost instantly within the shadows I saw a blacker shadow move. For a moment I thought my imagination was playing tricks upon me, for there was no wild creature on the North American continent that could be so tall as this, and then I knew that I was looking

upon the colossus of that rather extensive hemisphere—a lordly and full-grown moose.

Slowly, with the hesitancy of all its kind, it emerged from the wood and stood upon the gravelly shore. It was less than thirty feet from me, and everything conspired to make it seem more huge. The gray mists formed a background behind it. The weird light and my fevered imagination all played their part. The creature appeared to be ten feet tall.

I had seen moose before. On several occasions in Quebec we had paddled up within gunshot of them as they fed along the shores, and this was the third one I had seen within three days, but never before had I been as close as this to one of them. As yet no fluke of wind had warned it of the presence of man. It stood, proud and regal, broadside to me as it gazed out across the mists of dawn. It was a bull that, four months later, could cause any hunter's heart to stir with envy. Like all the rest of its sex it had shed its antlers sometime during the previous winter, but already the new set was beginning to grow. I could see them, bulbous protrusions that were each nearly the size of my fist, pushing upward through the coarse hair of the massive head. The bell, a curious appendage of skin and hair that hung from beneath its lower jaw, was as long as my forearm. As it stood there before me, I gauged it weighed—if my judgment is of any value—not less than a thousand pounds.

Unmoving as a bronze statue, it remained thus for long seconds, then it waded out into the lake until the water reached its knees and, lowering its head awkwardly, drank noisily from the crystal water.

I recall distinctly that several emotions gripped me. I wanted to arouse Chet and let him share the spectacle. I longed for my camera and a bit of sunlight. I knew the hunter's urge to look down a rifle barrel that pointed just back of those powerful shoulders—not to pull the trigger, but merely to line it up and speculate concerning the results if I did pull it.

What I did was to grope around on the ground beside me until my fingers closed over a good-sized stone, for, after all, men are but boys at heart. Slowly, carefully, I drew my arm back, and when the creature finished its drinking and raised its head aloft, I let fly at him with all the speed my cramped position would allow. I hope I could have done better with the rifle, because the stone fell short and a bit to the right. It struck the water with a glorious splash, but if I had expected to see the moose dash madly away I was disappointed, for it did not so much as turn its head. Born in that lonely wilderness and quenching its thirst from hundreds of lakes and streams, it had seen too many leaping trout to be alarmed by even so lusty a splash. I groped again, found another stone and, profiting by my first error, let fly once more.

Figuratively, the shot was a bull's-eye, although literally it was as far removed from the eye as it was possible to be and still be a direct hit, for the missile struck the creature fairly in the southernmost portion of its anatomy, and it produced results far beyond my fondest dreams. With a startled snort, the moose leaped directly ahead, then wheeled and, with its great splay hoofs churning the waters into a creamy froth, plunged up the bank and disappeared in the forest.

Instantly thereafter there was a movement behind me, and Chet thrust his head out from the tent. His black hair was rumpled, his startled eyes were wide.

"What in . . ."—in his excitement he designated a place that must remain unmentionable—"was that?"

"It was a bull moose," I said. "I shot him."

"You what?" His warden's instinct was aroused in a moment. "You did what?"

"I shot him," I reiterated, "three times. Imaginatively with my camera, theoretically with a rifle, and literally with a good solid rock. I've sure had an interesting morning."

He regarded me gravely for a moment, then he grinned. "Boy," he said, "I don't know whether you are aware of it or not, but you were taking a bit of a chance. Suppose he had decided to run in this direction?"

"I'd have been all right," I assured him. "I could have rolled out of the way."

"Oh, yeah. Well, how about me? I was in the tent."

"That's all right," I told him. "You wouldn't have been in it long. Not after the moose came in."

Jordan Lake

Were it not for the winds that have a perverse habit of springing up in open spaces, even in a day of apparently dead calm, I'd choose lakes every time for a canoe route, for they possess one decided advantage over streams. On one of the latter, the voyager is obliged to follow its vagrant and wholly irresponsible wanderings, which oftentimes become so confused that one can look back as he rounds an abrupt bend and see himself just emerging from another. Mark Twain said of such streams that they should be required to explain themselves, and he was right. Miles, especially if one is traveling upstream, are hard won, at least so far as a beeline is concerned, and a strenuous day's paddling along the serpentine meanderings of any stream that flows

66

through a flat country may find the traveler less than ten miles from the spot upon which he camped the previous night. But when one's route lies along a chain of lakes, if wind is not a factor, he may travel a straight course, and then the miles slip easily and quickly past. I am sorry that time is an element which enters into most of my affairs, and that schedules are a necessary evil on a wilderness trip. I'd like to strike out just once, neither knowing nor caring where I was going or how long I would stay. I would follow a lake route then, and when the whitecaps started their rolling I would go ashore and let them roll to their heart's content.

It required the combined effort of two experienced canoemen to make any sort of progress in heavy weather, and unfortunately Chet and I were both bowmen. A better man than I in either end of the craft, he nevertheless frankly acknowledged his feeling of inferiority while in the stern.

We got along famously, though, for he had not only been in the park for several years but he had used his power of observation. On more than one occasion while outlining the day's trip he would accurately call the turn on the condition in which we would find several lakes that we must cross. I don't know why one lake should be boisterously rough while at the same time another, lying only a mile distant and equally exposed to the wind, should be almost dead calm, but I know that it is true. I have witnessed the phenomenon on more than one occasion, and we proved it again on this trip, although neither of us learned the answer.

"The next one will be rough," Chet would say, or vice versa, and lo and behold it would be exactly as he said. It can be explained, no doubt, but not by me.

Chet was not only a keen observer but he also possessed the

happy faculty of being able to paint word pictures. He would describe a lake or turbulent cataract so accurately that when we came upon it I would have the feeling that I had seen it previously, and the anticipation of being able to pick out the distinctive spots along our route lent zest to the wearying labor.

Not so pleasant, though, was my anticipation of Jordan Lake, for while we were yet three days removed from it Chet began expressing the wish that we might hit it during a flat calm. Pressed for a reason, he admitted that Jordan was always rough, and he reiterated it several times daily thereafter. Consequently, I was prepared for what we encountered when we emerged from the mouth of the river and entered the lake.

Almost circular in shape, it stretched before us for a distance of six miles, and it was a welter of flying spume and dancing whitecaps. We had entered from the northern end and our objective was the easternmost point, but a straight course across the lake was impossible, for a mighty wind blew from the west.

It was my suggestion that we work down through the comparative calm of the lee shore to the western side of the lake and hold up there with the hope that the wind might ease up later in the afternoon. Then with a following breeze, we could skim easily and quickly across. To this he agreed, and sunset found us with supper eaten, the dishes washed and repacked, and the canoe trimmed and ready. Presently the wind lulled. It did not cease but it sharply diminished in volume. The angry muttering of the tossing waves changed to a soothing murmur and the whitecaps disappeared as though by magic. I looked questioningly at Chet.

"I think it will be all right," he said. "There's only one place— the narrows between a headland and an island—that we need worry about. It will be rough there, but not too rough."

We pushed the canoe out, stepped in, and struck off toward the dim and distant shore. The following wind was still blowing crisply from the west, and with its help we danced merrily along, trying but never quite succeeding to match the pace of the hurrying waves.

Big lakes, especially in the season of electrical storms, are always dangerous for canoe travel, for a sudden squall can lash the quiet waters to frenzy in a matter of moments, but I felt no anxiety on that score. They had told me that in addition to the boon of no hot days that particular section of the country never knew a thunderstorm. Driving seaward from the New Brunswick coast, they invariably disintegrated above the Bay of Fundy and had no time to rally their forces ere they were again swept to sea.

Consoling myself with that thought I bent to the paddle, and we were well out in the center of the lake when I heard a low and ominous rumble behind us. I looked back, and there, spreading its awesome bulk against the western sky, was the blackest shower cloud upon which I had ever looked.

Beneath me the canoe surged ahead as Chet poured his reserve energy into his paddle stroke, and I did the same. We instinctively knew that this was to be a race against time and that the time would be short. Three miles of open water lay before us and that meant that we needed nearly thirty precious minutes. Would that many be allotted to us? I looked back again. The cloud was nearer—much nearer—and it had assumed an indigo hue that meant only one thing. Wind! I did not look back again. A backward glance would cost a paddle stroke, and they were too precious to be wasted. Far behind us we could hear a steadily rising murmur that we knew to be the sound of tumbling white-caps. We drove the canoe hard and we drove it fast, but the wind caught us just before we reached the narrows.

How foolish we are to dread anything the future may hold. It was proved to me then. Before us surged a nasty cross chop, setting from the island toward the headland, but even as we approached it the wind, hurrying before us, caught it and straightened it out into smooth, easy swells through which we drove like nobody's business.

Ten minutes later we beached the canoe on the shore of a quiet cove on the mainland. We pitched the tent in a pouring rain, but Chet was humming happily. There was something hauntingly familiar about the tune. I listened and then memory awakened. He was singing "Way over Jordan, Lord."

Lunch on the Roseway

I WISH I KNEW its botanical name, but for want of it, or for a better means by which to identify it, I will refer to it as "waterbush." Sitting as I was in the bow seat of the canoe, the shrub stretched for an eighth of a mile on either side, at exactly eye level, and every branch was a glorious flaming pink. One's first reaction was to drive the canoe into it, step out, and gather an armful of it and revel in its flawless color.

Instantly, though, a warning flashed in my brain, a bell ringing loudly and clearly from a nameless little corner in southern Maine five hundred miles away. The time was October, and I was toting a shotgun and shooting ducks, or, if you demand accuracy, shooting *at* the little bluewing teal which traded back and forth between two small ponds which were connected by a lazily flowing brook.

There was no earthly reason for thinking so, but it occurred to me that my chances would be better if I crossed the brook. The decision, when I made it, involved three choices. I could go around the edge of either pond, or, for my third choice, I could go straight across through the waist-high grass that spread for a hundred yards on each side. I had no thought of danger. My one concern was that I might find a spot in the shallow brook where I could cross without going over the tops of my ten-inch shoepacs. I started across.

It was interesting from the very first step I took. Old grasses had long since rotted down and lush green ones had taken their place. The sensation was that of walking on a carpet that was six inches thick. The water came up around my ankles, but I kept steadily on, my eyes watching for approaching ducks.

Something, a slight nausea, perhaps, caused me to look down. Between me and the bank, which was still a hundred yards away, the grass was undulating like waves of the ocean. My footsteps, timed in unison, were building up a storm over a peat bog which, for all I knew to the contrary, may have been a hundred feet deep.

Don't tell me there is no such thing as self-levitation. I know better. I didn't *turn* around. I *floated* around, and I never once touched *terra firma* until I was safely over it.

Now, from the niche in which it had been lying more than a decade, that warning bell rang, and memory came surging back. I am led to wonder how many other men somewhere in the world have taken that last fatal step. But to return to my knitting.

Chet and I were paddling steadily along through fifth lake in the Roseway chain and we were nearing the end of the eight-day circle which had taken us around the perimeter of Tobeatic Park to our starting point on the Shelburne River. My watch had been under water too many times to expect accuracy from it, but my stomach corroborated Chet's timepiece, and we bent a little harder to our paddling.

Our situation was an unusual one for that occasion, for we were looking for a bit of sand or gravel beach on which to lay a small cooking fire, but those interminable waterbushes grew to the very edge of the stream, and Chet, a careful conservationist as well as a warden, would take no chances with fire.

A half hour later the sluggish stream quickened, we swept around an abrupt bend and a few feet of gravel beach lay before us.

We had been together for a week, and a pattern of living had gradually emerged. I pulled the bow of the canoe up on the shingle and picked up my fly rod. Chet dug the frypan from the kit and began gathering little scraps of dry driftwood for the fire.

"Trout?" I asked.

"Sure," he said, and I flicked ten feet of fly line out into the hurrying water.

"Whammo!"

Chet crouched at the water's edge, net in hand, and waited for me to lead the battler within reach. I did so and he scooped it up, rapped it over the head, and started cleaning it, but before he had finished the first cut I had another trout, a twin, waiting at the net. He scooped that one up also, and I looked at him inquiringly. He looked at the pair of fish, already seeming to savor their succulent richness, then raised a bloody finger aloft.

74

"One more," he said, exactly as he would have ordered it in a fish market. With equal unconcern, I led it to his feet.

I wonder occasionally how many times we would have had to try before we could have duplicated that instance anywhere in the States.

Rossignol the Untamed

SWING AND DIP, SWING and dip, drawing the paddle noiselessly out from the quiet river, burying it deeply again and applying power to it with a shoulder surge that had eight days of muscle-hardening toil behind it. The pace was both smooth and fast, although we had been keeping it up for hours, for this was the last day. More than one hundred miles of wilderness trail lay behind us, and only a short stretch of river and a bit of Lake Rossignol lay before. The canoe danced merrily, as though it knew the journey was nearly ended. It was lighter by far than when we started out, for Chet had figured the supplies with an accuracy that was uncanny. There was enough flour left for one more

76

batch of pan bread, and enough bacon to fry for one more mess of trout, but that was all. Not even a can of milk left for coffee. The great woods had added something to our appetites that no amount of ordinary toil could accomplish, and despite the labor of portages and the hard miles we had won only at the expense of perspiration-soaked clothing, there was a fullness at my waist-band that had not been there a week previously.

It was good to be coming home. There was not a moment of the trip to which I could not look back with pleasure, but home ties grow stronger when one has been beyond all means of communication for a week. So many things can happen in only a moment of time.

Lightened though it was of food, the canoe was nevertheless freighted with far more valuable things. The precious rolls of film, save for the one in the camera, were all exposed. The fly book was no longer immaculate. Instead, a hundred frayed and battered flies reposed within it, and on some future winter's evening when the north wind drove us closer to the friendly flames they would tell again their stories of the herculean battle they had fought. Securely rolled within my pack were a half-dozen birchbark patterns of trout in excess of three pounds in weight that I had taken, and the outer one measured nineteen and one-half inches from tip to tip. My notebook was filled to the last page, and a thousand memories crowded for first place in my remembrance. Yes, truly we were still freighted with tangible and wholly delightful things.

We drove on and at last, above the quiet ripple of the parting waters at our bow, I heard the distant murmur of rapids.

"It's the last of the white water," Chet said. "Rossignol's just ahead."

We rounded a bend and there it lay before us, a fast but easy pitch with plenty of water and only a few patches of white. Beyond it where the waters quieted again after their last hurrying rush, the broad expanse of the lake lay like an immense sheet of glass, with not so much as an errant wind flaw to ruffle its surface.

We drove straight ahead, for neither of us would brook the delay of a carry now. The current seized us and bore us on, while we paddled with even more vigor in order to maintain the necessary steerage way to avoid any obstacle that might suddenly confront us. It was over in a breathtaking moment and we were on the lake. Six miles across a tiny corner of it, then the short haul up the Shelburne and our journey would be done.

I said to Chet, as we drove onward across the lake, "Is Rossignol always like this? I never saw a lake so large that was so calm."

He said: "It's as unpredictable as a woman's fancy. It's a bad lake."

We crossed it and worked up the Shelburne just as dusk was falling. I dislike the twilights that come just before the parting of the ways. Better the rosy morn and a new sun shining in the east when the time approaches in which friends must part. I had known Chet but little more than a week but I had grown to like him immensely. We had so many common interests that helped draw us together. I knew that I would go back to Nova Scotia again, but the odds were great that when I said goodbye to Chet on the morrow I would be seeing him for the last time. That thought was uppermost in my mind when I rolled into a bunk in the base camp that night. I slept poorly because of it.

When we arose in the morning the wind was blowing—not in those squally puffs that had stirred Jordan Lake to frenzy, but a steady and relentless pressure that belied the power behind it. Only by the trees could one gauge its intensity. They had bent sharply before it and stayed thus, at an acute angle, while their trunks quivered as though ague-ridden.

"How will Rossignol be this morning?" I asked Chet.

He pushed the boiling coffeepot to the back of the stove and flipped the bacon skillfully from the frypan before he answered. "Plenty rough," he replied.

I thought there was an unaccustomed haste to his movements, and it was even more noticeable as we hiked down the two-mile trail to the Paper Company's wharf where our launch was tied. His four-foot stride proved to be too much for me after a while and I called a halt.

"What's your great hurry?" I protested. "You act as though you were anxious to get rid of me."

He grinned. "I'm anxious to catch the Company boat," he said. "It's bigger than ours."

There was food for thought in the simple statement, for the park boat was a twenty-footer—Lunenburg built, with a breadth of beam designed to stand any sort of weather. I wondered about it until we came in sight of the lake; then I knew the reason for Chet's anxiety. Thoughtful souls had pulled our boat high and dry far up upon her mooring slip. The Company boat, with two men already casting off her mooring lines and two more fending her off with sturdy pickpoles, was trying desperately to vault the wharf that stood five feet above the water's normal level. But for them, I think the boat would have made it, for although the wharf lay in a sheltered cove, the waves rolled across its planking knee deep.

A fifth figure, bent above the motor housing, straightened at

Chet's hail, looked up, and waved a hand in acknowledgment. We hurried down, tried for a minute to catch a lull in the waves, then waded out, tossed our duffel aboard, and vaulted in. The boatman pressed the starter, the wharfmen pushed mightily with their poles, the engine caught, and we were off.

The boat was a thirty-footer with a nine-foot beam, but as we rounded the point and stood out into the open water it seemed as puny as had our canoe on Jordan. The waves, racing toward us before that driving wind, seized upon it and tossed it about as though it were a bit of cork.

The skipper, a redheaded seadog from Yarmouth, perched on the edge of the engine housing and rode it out with the easy grace of a cowpuncher on a bucking broncho. His cheek bulged over an immense quid of tobacco with which he seemed to pre-serve his miraculous balance, for he shifted it repeatedly from one jowl to the other and spat copiously and promiscuously in all directions.

I am convinced he had the longshoreman's natural aversion to city "sports" and a particular aversion to me, for I caught him eyeing me reflectively. A moment later he let the boat fall off a trifle downwind, then brought her back into a roller at so precise an angle that a bucket of water hit the exact spot where I crouched beneath the lee rail. He must have had some experience in wing shooting, for although I shifted my position again and again and even dodging whenever he repeated the maneuver, he never once failed to score a direct bull's-eye. Ere we had prog-ressed a mile I resembled nothing so much as a drowned musk-rat, but not until I stood up and took it like a man did he desist. I cherish no resentment, though. He was a better sailor than I and he brought us safely across the roughest fresh water on which I ever looked.

I came back after we had climbed out and stored our duffel in the car, to gaze again upon the fury of Rossignol, the Untamed. Nine days ago it had beamed coyly at me. Now in a wild frenzy it lashed and tore at its barriers and shouted its hoarse challenge to all who would defy it. I thought it was a fitting symbol of all the wild and beautiful and untamed land I was leaving behind.

My Nova Scotia

"Yus," said Angus McPhee, as he rubbed his bare and bony knees and stretched them gratefully toward the fire that burned on neighbor Ainslie's grate. "Yus, I hae na doot we'll find it harrud for a year or twa, but Margie and I ha' made up our minds— or Margie has, which amainst to the same thing—and we're gooin'."

"The Heilands are not what they were," Bruce Ainslie sighed. "Pairrich for the bairns is mair deeficult to come by, and it's weel nigh eempossible to save even a wee bit the noo. Ye'll fare better in Quebec, na doot."

Angus McPhee also sighed. "A lang, harrud trip," he said,

82

"but the hardest is the pairtin' between friends. We'll miss you muckle and aft, neighbor."

"Ah weel." The bony Scot tried to view the matter philosophically. "Life is made of pairtin's. We'll meet again beyond, na doot. An, noo we'll hae a wee drappie for the sake of auld lang syne."

So it was that in the spring of 1811 the McPhees left the bonny banks of Clyde to take up a homestead for themselves in the province of Quebec. The voyage was an ill-starred one. Adverse winds beset them. Pestilence broke out, and the pirate, Death, boarded the ship and took his heaviest toll from the children. Two of the McPhee bairns were sewed in canvas and lowered into the deep.

Fifty days out, a terrific norther swooped down. Helpless, under bare poles, the tiny schooner drifted until it was hundreds of miles off course. When the storm was over and the sea had calmed, the ship began to limp its way back. Thirty days later, battered, beaten, but still afloat, it crept into the harbor of Yarmouth, Nova Scotia. Now that the bairns were gone, life had lost its charm, and one place was as good as another in which to spend their remaining days. Why go on to Quebec when Nova Scotia land was available? Going ashore, they acquired an ox team, loaded their meager goods on it, and struck off.

The parting of the neighbors in Scotland had produced an unexpected result, for it sowed the seeds of discontent in the hearts of the Ainslies. They had heard that the new Scotland was fairer than Canaan, a land of fertile fields and fair forests, where nature provided for every need. They talked it over, counted their pennies, and then booked passage for Nova Scotia.

Courageous indeed is the chronicler who dares to write facts. I know what will be my lot if I set down the plain and simple truth, but here it is; cross my humble heart.

Safely landed, the Ainslies inquired as to the best part of the province in which a loyal subject might acquire a King's grant. On being told that it lay along the banks of the Shubenacadie River, they embarked again in a small boat, worked their way up the Bay of Fundy, past towering Blomidon, and when Bruce Ainslie stepped ashore from the laden bateau and made his way up through a little clearing to a newly erected and crude log house, the first hand he grasped was that of Angus McPhee.

Of course the McPhees were blessed with a daughter, and of course the Ainslies had a son, else I, a century and a half later, would not be writing this. I owe them much, those ancestors of my mother, for they left me more than they knew. No miserly King's grant that can be measured in acres or miles, but a royal empire of level prairie and rolling hills, of rippling lakes and white-capped ocean, of turbulent tides rushing irresistibly inward, and of silvery rivers running down to the sea.

In this domain of mine the lordly moose treads the dim aisles of the forest, the whitetail deer flashes its warning signal as my scent reaches its nostrils. The black bear roams the ridges, while the industrious beaver carpenters build their dams across many a brawling brook or turbulent stream. Ducks and geese rear their young in the muskegs, unmolested by all except the sly raven, and mink and otter glide quietly along only to vanish abruptly when they catch the gleam of our canoe paddles. From the mighty deep the lordly salmon come in the spring to bore tirelessly up through the rivers to the spawning beds, while trout leap joyously in the riffles or feed in the quiet pools.

In this enchanted land I was privileged to roam on occasion,

84

and although I would forever be an alien, I learned to love the place as though it were my own. In those halcyon days I learned to like oatmeal porridge, to roll my r's, to shear sheep, and to swear fluently on the Micmac tongue when I nipped a finger. Small wonder that the first sniff of the salt marshes gives me the feeling that I am going home.

There are not many places left in the east where one may catch brook trout that have no taint of a fish hatchery about them. It is still possible, however, to do so in Nova Scotia, for there are countless ponds and lakes and hundreds of miles of streams that are particularly suited to the needs of *Salvelinus fontinalis,* and relatively few of them are polluted by manufacturing waste. The long and narrow peninsula is almost entirely surrounded by the Atlantic, and for that reason the temperature in summer averages several degrees cooler there than in the eastern states.

This air-conditioning system works equally well in reverse, tempering the winter winds, and for that reason the freezeup occurs later in the fall, and the breakup earlier in the spring.

This happy condition means, of course, that the trout enjoy a longer active period in which they may feed and put on weight. As a general rule granite, or high country, produces the best fishing throughout the season, but the flatter reaches of the muskeg country harbor some real tackle busters early in the season, or later if the weather remains cool. I have taken magnificent trout from the Roseway in mid-June.

There is fair landlocked salmon fishing in a few lakes. The plantings have never succeeded as well as they have on the mainland, but who cares about landlock when trout are rising to a fly or, if it must be salmon, then make it the Atlantic variety, for practically every river in Nova Scotia is a potential salmon stream of sorts, although some are much more productive than others. The gods were kind to salmon fishermen when they laid out the rivers; by some quirk of fate the salmon runs occur at widely different times, so there is always a river or two that is definitely "hot" at the moment. As an additional aid to the fishermen a bulletin goes out via radio each day from opening date on April 1 until the season closes on October 14. The Clyde and Jordan rivers in Shelburne County are among the earliest, although the Medway and La Have are only a day or two behind.

If bigger fish are wanted, then the Margaree is undoubtedly the best bet, for it annually gives up salmon that it is not necessary to lie about. The largest one, if my memory serves me correctly, weighed in at 51½ pounds. There are no closed or leased waters anywhere in the province.

One of the highlights in fishing the Bluenose country is the run of sea trout that occurs on most of the salmon streams from early May to mid-July. These silver-plated beauties are brook trout that have run down to the sea to feed among the kelp beds for several weeks and then run back inland after a thorough cleanup in the salt water. When they are running they will take streamer flies readily, but some of the rivers are treacherous when the tide changes.

I am a fly-rod man, and wouldn't give a thin dime to hook any fish that a five-ounce rod wouldn't handle, but for those who like that sort of thing there is extra-good tuna fishing along the south shore.

All in all, I don't know of a place where one may get as many fishing thrills for his money as he can in Nova Scotia. It is God's country—and mine.

II / Maine

Down East

I WAS GROPING MY WAY close to the shore of Camden's Lake Megunticook just as dawn was breaking. The night had been unusually warm, and the super-heated air had caused a heavy mist to
hang close to the water, baffling my effort to relocate a rocky
point where I had taken a few good bass the previous day.

Then just ahead of me, from the impenetrable murk, I heard
the creak of an oarlock, followed by the soft thud of oars being
stored amidships. I let my boat drift, and presently I could make
out the form of what appeared to be an old, old man, stooping
over, holding an ancohor rope in his hands. He saw me at the
same instant, dropped the rope, shipped the oars, and with a lusty
pull vanished like a ghost into the fog.

Now here was a queer thing. My hope of ever winning a beauty contest had long since died, and yet I found it impossible to believe that my face, especially when seen through so dense a fog, could be so frightening as to cause even a stranger to flee in terror. There was no sound from shore which could have alarmed him. In fact, there was no shore for the moment. Only the outline of a giant slab of granite which I remembered as a landmark. A slab which ran in a roof-steep slant down into the water. The old fellow was certainly a queer one. "Tetched" in the head, most likely—as all fishermen are—only to a slightly greater degree.

The bass were kindly all day, but ever and anon the thought of that shy old-timer came back to bother me. Even when on the verge of slumber that night I found myself pondering over it. Why had he departed so hurriedly? Then, sometime in the wee small hours the answer came to me and brought me wide awake. The old fellow was going to anchor there, just off the granite ledge. He knew something about that particular spot which he did not intend to share with anyone else. The answer was obvious. I was on the lake again before dawn.

It was another foggy morning, but I found the ledge without too much difficulty, and backed water to stop the forward progress of the boat while I was still thirty feet from shore. I opened my tackle box, dug out a dipsy sinker, tied it to the leader on my fly line and let it run down into the depths, but before it touched bottom I felt it hit the granite wall and grate along it as it ran downward. I moved the boat a bit farther out and tried it again and once more it touched rock. I moved out another boat length, and this time the lead ran straight down and plunked into something soft and yielding. I brought it up, smeared it liberally with line dressing, lowered it to the bottom, and hauled it up once more. The grease was impregnated with sharp white sand, which told me surely that down there at the foot of the slanting ledge a spring was bubbling up, and that some of the big trout which were known to be in the lake would be cruising around the in-rushing cold water. I lowered the anchor and had just enough rope to reach bottom. There was, I estimated, about fifty feet of water beneath me.

I was looping a heavier leader to my line when I again heard the grating of oarlocks, and the shy stranger of yesterday morning slid in through the mists. He was startled when he saw me, and I caught the swift glance he shot at my anchor rope and shipped oars, but he did not speak. Instead, he rowed completely around me, then pulled in beside me.

"You're in the right place," he said, grudgingly. "You're in exactly the right place."

I assured him that, if I was, it was a pleasant thing to know.

"It's right where I always anchor," he informed me, and there was a touch of melancholy in his voice. "Right exactly where I always anchor."

"Well," I said, "tie up alongside. There's room for both of us." But he shook his head. "I'll move down a bit," he said, and did so while I lowered a worm-draped hook to the bottom and then rasied it a foot or two.

I think I had bobbed the bait up and down for ten minutes before I had the first touch. It was a light one, but as I held the line between my fingers I could feel a faint vibration as something mouthed the bait. Then it clamped down on it and started to move away. I set the hook, picked up the rod, and knew immediately that I had a good fish on, for he took line in strong rushes which the fly rod could not check.

In the other boat the old-timer was standing erect, waving his

arms and imploring me by all I held sacred to drop the rod, grab the line, and haul the fish in hand over hand. "You'll lose him that way," he shouted. "You'll lose him sure as fate. Haul him in quick."

I advised him to sit down and take it easy. It looked as though I was going to be busy for a few minutes, and if he jumped around and fell out of the boat he would get mighty wet before I got around to pull him in. He crouched down on a thwart but he couldn't remain silent, "They're big trout," he squealed in a high, cracked voice. "The only way to land 'em is to haul 'em in fast. Git a holt on that line and pull him in."

I told him that I didn't particularly care whether I landed the fish or not if it would only give me a ten-minute fight. He couldn't understand it, but with the exception of numerous mouthings and splutterings he remained comparatively quiet until I had the fish near the surface where I could see it. What I had told him about not caring had been the strict truth up to that moment, but when the trout rolled so that I could see the size of him, I knew that I very much wanted to see him inside my net. I reached for it, but when I shook it out the old-timer had another spasm which put all his previous efforts to shame.

"No! NO!" he screamed. "You'll lose him that way just as sure as time! Pull him in!"

In his excitement he tripped over an unseen something in the bottom of his skiff, and only a miracle saved him from going overboard. I yelled to him to sit down again, put a bit of extra pressure on the rod, and slid the net under as pretty a two-pound trout as one could hope to see. It was thick and deep, and beautiful beyond words. I held it up for the old-timer's approval and he breathed a gusty sigh of relief.

"Didn't believe you could do it," he said. "The only way to handle—" He gave a tremendous yank on the line he was holding, and his face lit up like a rising full moon.

"Got one!" he yelled, and began hauling in furiously, hand over hand, the line running across the gunnel to form a getaway setup that would have shamed a ten-year-old boy. It was my time to get excited.

"Keep him away from the boat," I shouted. "Keep him an arm's length away. If he hits the rub rail he'll get off." But the old man paid no heed to my cries. Watching, fascinated, I saw a mighty trout come to the surface in a smother of foam, hook its nose fairly under the rub rail, give a mighty flop, and plunge back into its element, a free and probably wiser fish.

My sympathy goes out to anyone who loses a fish like that, but for a few minutes I feared for the old man. He moaned and groaned and bewailed the fate that had dogged his footsteps all through life, and adjured me by all I held sacred to never divulge to anyone the secret of the spring as long as we both should live. I pledged my honor and have kept my vow inviolate until now, for the old man has long since gone to angle in celestial springs from celestial boats that need no rub rails.

My pledge, though, concerns Megunticook only. There are numerous underwater ledges and drop-offs that furnish some of the best bass fishing in Maine. Bass are plentiful, and some of them reach a respectable size. To one of the latter I have proposed many a toast, although our acquaintance has been brief. The events leading up to the incident can be briefly told. I was combing a bit of marsh for fly-rod-size frogs for bass bait, when a big, old, green grandfather of a frog found his way into my net and, eventually, into my bait can.

94

The bass that day were small, but they were accomplished bait stealers; however, I continued to feed them small frogs until the little fellows were down to their last half dozen. Then I noticed old "gramp." Sober reflection told me that he was no fly-rod lure. Reason said to toss the creature overboard, but I remembered that there was a new twenty-four-pound test line in my tackle box, and that it was wound on a reel that could be attached to a heavy rod. I told reason to go hang, rigged the outfit up with a heavy leader and outsize hook, and tossed the whole thing overboard. I had neither hope nor expectation that anything would touch the bait. Occasionally in the spring a few big salmon were taken there, but not on meadow frogs. I promptly forgot all about it and went back to my bass fishing.

Time passed —an hour or more—and then I noticed that the boat had swung around so that the heavy line slanted toward the bow. Ten minutes later it had turned the other way. Then it began to move straight out from the boat. Then the reel clicked once—twice—and the handle moved a fraction of an inch. It moved again, another fraction. Then it snarled "yah—yar!" and the reel handle became a blur. A hundred times since then I have cursed myself for my folly. All I needed to do was to pick up my rod, set the hook, and see what happened. Instead of that, I reached down, took the line between thumb and forefinger, clamped down hard on it and gave my wrist a twist. If I had hooked into a submarine the effect would have been the same. The new line parted as easily as though it was a cotton thread, and I was left to ponder the question that can never be answered. Was it a record salmon or giant bass that took the grandfather frog? I will never know! I will never know!

95

Flies, etc.

WHAT IS THE BEST all-around fly for trout? I have spent many futile hours in an attempt to solve that problem, but my research has paid off in the end. Considered from every angle, and forgetting moon phase and sidereal radiation, the best fly to use anywhere east of Suez is the one the angler is just taking from his fly book. Let me say to the skeptic that I can cite many a well-documented case in proof of my contention if he demands it. Take, for instance, the Bog Brook affair. Let me say right here that I have a very special affinity for this wonderful man-trap of a brook with its beaver-created pools—an affinity which dates back to the days when baiting ducks was legal. Memory stirs, and a

quarter of a century vanishes as though a curtain had been un-
rolled.

It is July. The last firecracker has exploded, the last flag has
been waved, the last senator has viewed with alarm, and nothing
but work stares me in the face. There is one remaining loophole,
though, one avenue of momentary escape from the drudgery that
I am facing. I reach for it as a drowning man grasps a Mae West.
Because of the parades and other patriotic activities it is doubtful
if any of the die-hard, last-day trout fisherman have flicked a fly
into the brook's upper pool. I threw my fishing gear into the car
trunk, backed out of the driveway, and drove casually away.

The time was later than I thought, for the sun was sliding
down toward the distant mountain and the western edge of the
pool was in deep shadow. It is a deceptive sort of pool, wider
than its fifty feet would lead one to believe, and deeper than any
pool has a right to be when one is wading waist-deep after a bro-
ken-winged mallard.

But it is a trout pool, nevertheless, a meeting place where redspots rendezvous in October before they crowd up the tributary
brooklets to spawn. Full many a time our early-season fish and a
late-season fisherman have crossed swords over the quiet water of
the pool and stirred it to its depths with thrust upon thrust and
parry upon parry.

I was thinking such thoughts as these when I jointed my rod
and cast a speculative eye at a neighboring maple limb that might
prove to be a hazard to my back cast, then flicked a high-riding
Palma Belle into the pool.

Instantly a trout rose to it, coming up with a surge that started
the concentric rings rolling on their way to shore; but it had no
intention of taking my offering.

For a few seconds I let the fly ride, moving it carefully, an inch at a time, but the old fellow would have no part of it. Reluctantly I reeled in, selected another pattern and tied it on, then waited for a long five minutes before I offered it again.

Exactly as it had done before, the trout rose to it, but again with no intention of taking. I changed flies again and again.

It may or it may not be true that the trout knew what he wanted, but it is definitely true that he had a very clear image of the flies he did not like. I changed them repeatedly, and at each offering he rose once and once only. Then I got careless with my back cast and hung my fly on the maple limb. I wanted the fly, for it was of a pattern I had not tried, so I climbed the tree, broke off the limb, and tossed it down.

To most readers the remainder of the little story will sound apocryphal, but it is nevertheless a fact. Another fly was caught in the limb. I rescued it, tied it on, offered it to the trout, and he took it solidly and surely on the first cast.

There at last was the evidence which I sought. There was no need to call judge and jury to decide. The fly, a faded, washed-out, red-tinted, half-sized streamer, was indisputably the correct one to use in the big pool. I went home and tied a half-dozen copies of the thing, so that in the event of a concerted attack on them I would be sure of saving at least one for a sample, but it didn't work out that way. I carried those flies for years and years on both sides of the border, and to the best of my knowledge and belief not one of them has ever taken a trout anytime anywhere.

What other proof do I need? If you desire still more I'll cite to you the fact that is usually overlooked in sifting the evidence: I have absolutely no proof that I was casting to the same fish every time. For all I know to the contrary, I might have taken a dozen fish with almost any other fly in the book.

Are you still unconvinced? Then let's move north a hundred and fifty miles to the Upper Grandbank pool on Kennebago River. It was one of those disappointing days to which fishermen sometimes find themselves subjected. There were plenty of fish in the pool. Look almost anywhere in its hundred-foot length and you could see the dimples made by rising fish, but the rises were desultory. Occasionally a small fish would take an offering, but it would take little interest in the resulting fight. Fishing, it seemed, had gone to the dogs, and I reluctantly followed them ashore to rest a while.

Then the warden came in for a license checkup. After it was over we sat on the dry gravel and talked of this and that and principally about the lack of interest shown by the trout. I opened a fly book and we pawed over patterns which might or might not be the answer. At last he dug out a divided-wing, gray fly of my own tying and looked at it critically.

"Hum-m!" he said. "Here's an odd one! What is it?"

Blushingly, I told him that it was one of my night-born fancies. He wanted to know if it would work. The only way to answer that was to tie it on and pass the rod to him. He made a few casts that were something to watch with envy, but with an entire lack of resulting action. Then he passed the rod back to me.

There's one spot in the Gravelbank that appeals to me more than any of the others. Somewhere down near the lower end there is some kind of unidentifiable minor obstruction, and over it the water seems to bulge a fraction of an inch and quicken its pace an equal amount. From shore it is not visible unless one knows exactly where to look, but trout lie there in the quickened current, and some of them have taken a fly of mine.

I waded out into the pool, a good thirty feet above the bulge, purposely casting a few feet short, then shook out loose line and let the fly ride down over the bulge.

A good trout took it, and by good in this instance I mean a trout an inch or two more than a foot in length. It was the best fish I had seen come out of the pool all day. I almost wanted to keep it, but I turned it loose, looked at the fly, and made another cast to the same spot. Immediately a trout took it, hitting it hard and authoritatively, and when I set the hook he showed me that he had a will of his own. When the flurry was over I prepared to cast again but noticed that a wing was missing on my poorly tied fly. I thought of changing it but decided to try one more cast. Exactly as before, still another trout met it on the bulge and took the tattered relic.

I looked at the fly, and the other wing was gone, but it made no difference. Whatever went over that bulge was grist for their mill and they took it enthusiastically.

Then the yarn body began to unwind. I broke off the dangling two inches and a trout leaped for it. I broke off more yarn and tried again. Same results. On the last cast I made the yarn was held by a single knot, and when I removed the hook it came out absolutely bare, but it had brought in eleven fine trout.

It is my contention that in addition to the first three I took when the fly was unmarred, it had taken at least eight different trout.

If from that scrambled mess of facts anyone can pick a surefire winner for Kennebago's Gravelbank pool, I would like to have his telephone number.

Still another instance comes to mind. It is mid-October, on the same Bog Brook, and I approach the pool in the same manner that I had done before: carefully, one cautious step at a time, and with murder in my heart.

The fly rod, thoroughly dried and cased, was standing in its nook in the den, and in its place I was carrying a Model 12 Winchester 12-gauge. The big pool was a natural resting place for mallards and black ducks, and it was open season; hence my caution.

The night was darker than dark. It was even blacker than back, and not a single star twinkled over head. I was alone in a world in which there was not a single vestige of light. As I moved along, feeling out each step in the path before I bore my weight on it, I began to hear tiny sounds that came from the direction of the pool. The sound, as I came nearer, seemed to be continuous splashing, such as might be made by a hundred babies beating their hands together simultaneously in a hundred bathtubs. As blind as I was, I could tell that the pool was bulging with ducks. If the noise they made was a criterion by which I might judge their number, there were at least a thousand ducks taking their matutinal dip. My trigger finger itched uncontrollably. Time stopped. The hourglass refused to run and the blackness increased. Then, mysteriously, there was light in the east, a spear of red shooting up into the black void that was the sky. The clamor in the pool increased in intensity with the advent of a bit of light and I could see that the water was white with spray. What species of ducks they were I could not guess, but I vowed that I would find out, even if I had to potshoot one for a sample.

Then my laggard brain squeaked warningly, wheels rumbled and groaned, and I knew at last what was causing all the uproar.

From bank to bank for the length of the pool the water was literally white spray cast up by leaping trout. I do not even dare to guess how many they were. Neither do I dare to estimate their size, but I know that there was an unbelievable number of them and some of them were of an unbelievable size.

Why they leaped the way they did I have no way of knowing. Certainly they were not feeding, but it is equally certain that there were no obstructions which they had to leap over. If anybody should suggest that the story has grown with the telling I can merely say that it had ample room to grow. There were an awful lot of trout.

Kennebago

On an office wall at Grant's Camps at Kennebago Lake in Maine, there is a card so unique that it attracts and holds the attention of any fisherman who sees it. A fly is attached to the center of the card. Although still serviceable, it is a trifle battered, suggesting that it has fulfilled a dry fly's destiny. A neatly printed legend verifies the suggestion.

The legend briefly certifies that on a late June morning in 1954 the fly brought forty-one trout to net. It was a long time ago, but it is still an accolade to the man who tied the fly, as well as to the fisherman who used it; in addition, it indicates the trout potential in that wholly delightful country.

Of all the trout lakes in Maine, none is more legendary than Kennebago. A century or more ago natives of the little town of Rangely used to leave their own productive waters and make ox-team pilgrimages to the smaller lake in order that they might satiate themselves with red-spotted and red-fleshed Maine brook trout. Conditions have changed at Kennebago since then: a railroad has come and gone, a power dam has been erected, Prohibition wore an easily followed trail to the Canadian line; but despite all the changes, Kennebago remains much the same as it was a hundred years ago. Raising the water level caused a large flowage to build up between the larger and smaller lakes, and it has proved to be a vast rearing pool for myriads of fingerling trout.

Three quarters of a century ago, after several years of legislative manipulating, Maine sold hundreds of square miles of its wild lands to private interests. The furore that was made when starry-eyed pioneers found that a tightly knit organization held options on the entire tract would have made the Teapot Dome controversy seem like a mild altercation among a group of Girl Scouts. There is no doubt that the consummation of the deal required some shrewd finagling, and it is possible that, as some contend, several pocketbooks were substantially fattened thereby, but the long-term results have not been what the prophets of doom predicted. Instead, the vast woodland area is, in effect, a huge game sanctuary from which the outlying districts are continuously restocked. Within the area, scientific and up-to-date forestry is religiously practiced, while constant watch and modern fire-fighting equipment have kept that hazard down to a minimum.

Although the lumber companies have tight control over the

forest, they have no jurisdiction over the lakes, ponds, or navigable streams within their domain. Consequently, any resident of the state, or nonresident if he is properly licensed, has the right to fish any water, although the manner in which he reaches the water guarantees that the lakes will never be overfished. He may fly in, travel by boat or canoe, walk or hop in on a pogo stick, but he cannot, at least not in the Kennebago territory, drive his car on company roads without a permit.

A cynic would naturally say that any body of water so publicized and pounded through the years would not yield enough trout to scent up a frypan, and but for one happy circumstance they would be right.

The men and women who go to Kennebago—and some have not missed a season for a quarter century—are anglers who fish for the sport it affords. Many use barbless hooks, or hooks on which the barbs are bent down, and it is my guess that among the regulars ninety per cent of the fish are returned unharmed to the water. The few killers who occasionally find their way in learn to their surprise that accommodations are unavailable at the present moment nor are any expected at any future time.

If I said that a fisherman could go to any lake in Maine, at any time of his choice, and be sure of taking at least one fish, I should be guilty of exaggeration. So many factors of heat and cold, or wind and rain, of clouds and sunshine have their effects that a sorcerer with a crystal ball could not accurately picture the result. But if my future welfare depended upon my ability to take a mess of speckled beauties, I know of no place I should choose in preference to Kennebago.

There are certain seasons of the year when superlative sport may almost surely be had. The first one occurs immediately after ice-out. Then, at Great Sag, at the northern side of the lake, dace, coming in to spawn in the shallow water, are followed by big trout. The run lasts only a few days, but four-pound trout are not unusual there.

Immediately following this brief period the dace start running the mile-long stretch between Big and Little Kennebago. Here is stream fishing at its best. One may wade out in the Gravelbank Pool halfway up the river, and with the sun at one's back one may look down on dozens of beautiful fish. Stream fishing usually holds up until about June 10.

The highlight of the season is the trout convention which usually starts about the last week in June and extends until mid-July. It is during this period that the mayfly hatches occur, and if one is equipped with a goodly number of dry flies he may reasonably expect to catch trout until his arm tires. Although the fish taken at this period will average less than a pound in weight, others weighing two or three pounds are not uncommon. The secret, if there is one, lies in knowing when and where to fish.

For the man who still insists on taking trout in August there are several outlying ponds from which a man may take hundreds of eight- to nine-inch trout. Little Island Pond is a good example. The pond is crowded with fish, and that is probably the reason why they never grow more than a foot in length. Cold springs which are located in several places in the pond bring the fish to them by thousands as soon as the weather gets warm enough. The late Everett Greaton and I have taken and released more than a hundred trout on a blistering August afternoon.

Ten fish or 7½ pounds is the legal limit here, and it is usually easy to select ten take-home fish that will round out the weight limits. Here, as in all connected waters, only flies fished in the

coventional manner may be used. This rules out spinning and trolling gear.

One should remember that Kennebago is in the north country and Maine climate can be pretty rugged at times. Take double the amount of clothing you think you may need, and you will have no more than enough. Even in May, balmy spring weather may change to a howling gale in a matter of minutes and leave the ground white on the following morning.

If things slow up in August one can turn to landlocked-salmon fishing, for that is when they start running in the river below the powerhouse. There are several good pools, and after the season gets underway one is almost sure to pick up a fish or two during the middle of the week when most of the pools will be unoccupied. Incidentally, this is the stream that was favored by the dean of American flycasters, the late and incomparable Herb Welch.

I have fished Kennebago a goodly number of times. I hope to fish it a goodly number more. It's God's country up there.

Fisherman's Luck

I TRY TO BE COSMOPOLITAN in my choice of fishing partners, but one must draw the line somewhere and with extreme reluctance I have crossed ministers off my list. I dislike doing it, for I believe in most cases parsons are as good as regular people, although they are severely handicapped. Such ejaculations as "Oh, my" and "Dear me" are hardly adequate when a leader breaks or a good fish is lost at the net. There should be some special dispensation for a parson caught in such a predicament, and for all I know to the contrary there may very well be one. Under such circumstances I have known a clergyman to grow apoplectic and beg to be set ashore for just a little while.

But not my parson. I met my man at a Boy Scout jamboree. He was breaking eggs into a giant frypan, which was something any Boy Scout could do, but he was picking them up three at a time with his right hand, cracking the shells against the edge of a saucer which he held in his left, forcing them open with a clever twist of his thumb, and sliding them, with a sort of assembly-line motion, into the saucer for a quick check for an overripe specimen, and then, with the yolks still unbroken, sliding them into the sizzling frypan.

"Look, brother," I said. "Are you really doing that, or do I just imagine that you are? Why, the thing's impossible. It is a miracle. How did you learn to do it?"

"Working my way through college as a short-order cook," he said. "It required a lot of practice—with the other fellow's eggs. But miracles do happen. I'll tell you about one after we have taken care of the boys' inner needs."

So it was that later in the day when the tents were all set, and the fires had begun to twinkle along the sandy beach, that the parson told me the story that marked the beginning of a friendship which I still highly prize.

"I was plug casting for bass," the parson said, "and I had taken the boy with me. He's four, and has already shown some interest in fishing. I was a hundred feet out in the lake, casting toward shore when it happened. A backlash! The plug came back like a bullet. I didn't have time to move an inch before the plug with its treble hook struck the boy full in the face. He was screaming hysterically as I got to him and got him into my arms and held his hands, which were clawing for the plug. The hook, I could see, was buried in his eye.

"It was a minute before I realized what a predicament I was in. I had intended to make only a few casts and I had no pliers. I had to hold the boy's hands, and that left me only the other one with which to handle an oar. Did you ever try to row a boat with only one hand and one oar, and with a four-year-old boy screaming from pain? I tried it, and I'm telling you it can't be done. I prayed. Believe me, I prayed! And then the miracle happened. Doc Brown, our town doctor, had come out to fish for a half hour before going to his office. He heard the racket and came over. He had his tackle box along, and in a minute he had the hook out. It couldn't just *happen*. Something that was not mere chance took over in the next few seconds. The hook had pinned the upper and lower lids together over the eye without touching the eyeball."

That was the beginning of our friendship. The next spring, shortly after ice-out, we were on our way to the Rangeley Lakes country after landlocked salmon.

There was the merest suspicion of a breeze, and the little ponds we passed rippled in the April sunshine.

"The weather has settled at last," the parson said, but as we swung into the mountains a squall came roaring down the Sandy River Valley. A half hour later we ran into another one. When we reached Rangeley the lake was frothy with whitecaps, but the squall soon passed.

"That is the last one," the parson said, confidently. "See how clear it is in the west. Let's find a campsite, pitch the tent, and get something to eat. Then we'll go out and tie into a big one for supper."

It didn't work out that way. We alternated between casting, changing flies, and rowing to shore as another storm rolled down the lake. By the last glimmer of daylight we ate supper, but we ate beans instead of lordly salmon.

The parson was morose. While we were washing dishes he

paused suddenly, faced an imaginary audience, and with his magnificent voice fairly dripping sarcasm declared to the dripping
world:

"Yes, come to Maine, the sportsman's paradise. Maine with its
virgin forests and myriad waterways. Come to Maine, where the
woods teem with game and the waters abound with fish."

We went to bed early. My last waking thoughts, I remember,
were pleasing ones. Through the open tent flap I could see the
western sky. It was cloudless and star-flecked.

"Nice day tomorrow," I said, sleepily, but the parson was already snoring gently.

Sometime during the night I roused. There was a tremendous
hammering all about us, and it was bitterly cold. It took me a few
moments to realize that the roaring was caused by wind in the
trees, and the pounding was that of the waves on the rocky
shore. Dawn found us standing at the edge of the lake, staring
disconsolately at the turmoil of wind and water.

"Yes, come to Maine," the parson intoned. He had yet to
drink his first morning cup of coffee and was still cynical.

"Come on! Let's go fishing," he said.

"Where?" I asked.

"Quimby Pond. It is sheltered enough so we can fish it. No
salmon but some nice trout."

Quimby Pond is both well and favorably known, but it is very
shallow. Today the wind had stirred it to its depths, and it now
resembled fairly thick pea soup. Two hours of casting convinced
us that we were merely wasting our time. We got in the car
once more and drove to Rangeley village.

"We'll go into the sporting goods store," the parson said, "and
get some firsthand information. They must know of some se-
cluded spot where we can catch a fish or two."

The proprietor didn't know. "Poor season," he said. "Mighty poor. Don't know what would be a good bet for them, do you, George?"

George was one of the natives grouped around the big stove that was sending out a welcome warmth on that late April day. His glib manner convinced me that he was a member in high standing of the Ananias Club.

"There's some pretty fair fishing around here if you know just where to go," he said, "but when I want some real good fishing I drive south."

"South?" The parson's tone expressed incredulity. "How far south?"

"Oh, a hundred miles or so."

"In what locality?"

George did dome quick mental arithmetic in order to determine just how far south a hundred miles would carry him. "Half Moon Lake," he said.

"What does one catch there?"

I caught a flicker of amusement in the parson's eye. He had his trap set now, and was waiting for Geroge to blunder into it.

"Salmon, trout, and bass," said George. "Big ones, too. I was down there two weeks ago. Didn't get out on the pond until two hours before dark but I took the limit of salmon and trout and got two bass that weighed nine pounds."

"Well, well, well!" The parson's voice dripped honey. "Half Moon Lake, eh? I have a camp and a boat there. I shall fish with renewed interest from this time on. Thanks immensely for the information."

I hope I shall never forget the parson's hearty laugh as we went out. "He had the four points of the compass to choose from," he said. "It was a tough break for him when he chose south. Well, how do you like the idea of taking a basket of brook trout from the Sandy River? We should be able to catch enough to scent up the frypan."

"The idea is a good one," I agreed, "but I have the impression that parts of it are closed to fishing." I got out the law book and studied it. Sure enough, there it was: "The upper reaches of Sandy River from Higgin's Bridge to the Upper Falls shall be closed to all fishing for the period of five years."

"That's definite, isn't it?" said the parson. "Where is Higgin's Bridge?"

"Where are the Upper Falls?" I countered.

We met a native driving a two-horse team. "Where is it lawful to fish Sandy River, brother?" queried the parson.

"I don't know," the native said, helpfully. "Better ask the warden and get it straight."

"Where does he live?"

"Up at Strong. Keep straight ahead for about ten miles till you come to a village with two churches. You swing sharp around the Baptist church, and the warden lives—"

"Which one is the Baptist church?" I asked, but the parson gave me a dig in the ribs. "Don't be silly," he said. "It's the one nearest the water."

"Yep. That's it," said the native. "Built right on the bank of the river. Swing sharp around the church, and the warden lives in the second house after you go past Ed Tyson's place."

The warden, it developed, was away, so we took a chance and stopped at the next roadside pool. It was as beautiful a trout stream as can be found anywhere in Maine, and it was alive with trout just a hair short of the legal length. At sundown we gave it up and drove back to camp. In our baskets were just eight trout that a not too zealous warden would pass without measuring. We ate them for supper, supplemented by beans and pan bread, but no salmon.

I awoke in the morning with a sense of something lacking. For a moment or two I could not determine what it was, and then I knew. It was the utter stillness. Springing from the cot I looked out upon a different world. The branches of the trees were motionless. The lake in the early morning light was glassy smooth. There was a soft languorous warmth in the air. It was, in fact, the sort of morning that poets write about.

My ecstatic shout roused the parson and he came out, pajama-clad, to see what had happened. We did a jubilant war dance for a minute, then made a dash for our clothes. Ten minutes later, minus breakfast but plus a boundless enthusiasm, we were on the lake. Five minutes later, retrieving line carefully, the parson struck sharply, and the water parted as the hook slid home in the jaw of a leaping, tail-walking salmon.

That first fish was worth the cost of the entire trip. He fought, and the parson yelled, and pandemonium reigned as the four-pound fish staged its last battle. It was a typical landlock, bright with an almost metallic brightness, through which showed an irregular pattern of St. Andrew's crosses. That was the life!

Shortly afterward I caught the mate of the parson's fish, and before it had ceased its struggles the parson was fast to his second one. After a half hour without another strike the parson suggested that we go ashore, get breakfast, pack our outfit, and then come back and fish until noon.

"I really should be back early," he said. "I have to preach to-morrow morning, you know."

"Why not dig a sermon from the bottom of the barrow for

once?" I asked. But he would not agree to it. "It wouldn't be exactly cricket," he said, "to run in an old one." If he could have just two or three hours of quiet study that evening, he said, he would make out all right. We went ashore.

It was still too calm for good fly fishing, but about ten o'clock a breeze sprang up. An hour later there was a good ripple, and by twelve-thirty we had taken two more salmon. Then the smaller fish struck in, fish of around fifteen inches in length—too small to keep, but ideal for sport on a light fly rod. The Rangeleys are like that—either a feast or a famine, and this was the afternoon of the feast. Hours slipped by unnoticed, until all at once I saw that it was growing dark. The parson, too, was surprised, and begged for "just one more cast" before we quit. It had been a day to remember.

We had everything timed just right, for I rolled into the parson's yard just as the town clock was striking midnight. I had intended to drive straight through to my home in New Hampshire, but when I saw a vacancy sign at a motel a whim seized me and I took the room.

Next morning, with only a slight odor of fish permeating the air around me, I went to church. I wanted to hear the parson speak, and he came through fine. He spoke all about the miracle draught of fishes. It was a good sermon. It kept me awake, which was quite a miracle in its own right.

Camp Cooking

In my opinion cooking is as much a fine art as sculpture or painting. I would not go so far as to say it is a lost art, but I claim, and I know that millions of bicarbonate of soda addicts will agree with me, that while a can opener is all right in its place, it is a mighty poor substitute for a mixing spoon. Where can we find those red-jellied, flaky-crusty apple pies like Mother used to make, or such golden-topped biscuits and nut-flavored yeast bread as we knew in an era that has passed? Fortunate indeed is the man who knows the answer, for the great majority only know that it cannot be found in cans.

Camp activities and exercise in the open air are unparalleled tonics for the appetite, and fortunately they are also the best of digestive aids, for contrary to fiction not all outdoorsmen are good cooks. Man is not the spiritual creature he imagines himself to be. He may live on scenery and sunsets for a while, but the day will come when he longs for the fleshpots again. Then, if he awakens to find himself sitting bolt upright in the bunk, with his head bowed between his knees, and with two husky football teams scrimmaging in his stomach, he will know that once again he has made a bad choice in the matter of cooks.

In the north, men depend largely upon fats to furnish body heat, but in a more temperate area a man eats and is immediately conscious of a deep inner craving for lemons or pickled limes, or even a soothing draft from a vinegar cruet.

Bacon is the staple from which there is no escape. A man awakens with the odor of its frying in his nostrils, and crawls out of his tent to watch the guide cut countless other quarter-inch-thick slices from a seemingly endless supply. Not until a plate is heaped high with the flabby slices will he desist and begin to cook breakfast. The bacon is not breakfast. It is merely a curtain raiser to it, an appetizer that the guide bolts down just as a lesser man would nibble at a cracker.

On fishing trips fishermen eat fish—or at least I hope they do—and I long ago learned that when a man pledges himself to eat trout or salmon twice a day he will find that after the second day the thought of another meal will be slightly revolting. The reason, of course, is that he has been taking in fat faster than he can assimilate it. The surefire panacea is to skin the fish before cooking them. If they are too small to skin, bake them in a hot oven.

If it is landlocked salmon that you are cooking, plank it. Planking consists of splitting the fish down their backs and fastening them by their tails beside (and not over) the cooking fire. You'll be surprised to see how much oil drips out. If you bake them, put them on a rack.

Griddle cakes are a staple. Now with the advent of Teflon II it is no longer needful to use oil in either pan or batter. It puts to route the older guide's belief that the perfect pancake is one in which a lamp wick may be inserted and furnish light by which he may read through a long winter night.

Despite all I have said to the contrary, men are the world's best cooks. If woman had been left to her own devices, man would still be gnawing his breakfast off the shinbone of an ox and eating it raw to boot.

No one realizes more than I the risk I am running, both at home and abroad, in making a statement such as that. While I have never written purposely to please the ladies, I have carefully tried not to antagonize them; but now that the die is cast, I shall go bravely ahead, upheld by the sure conviction that truth will eventually prevail.

To man belongs the credit for creating almost all worthwhile inventions. Rubbing down a spear with a bit of rock, man learned that friction produced heat, and from that he evolved fire. Thawing a quarter of mastodon that he might more easily sink his incisors into it, he learned that burning improved flavor, and thus cooking was born.

Woman, sadly, has less imagination. Her masterpiece, no matter how delicious it may be, is usually only something that man has perfected.

On the other hand, man's search for perfection still goes on unchecked. He is forever experimenting in his endless quest for some new culinary triumph. Of course, his efforts are not always

crowned with success, for admittedly success is only achieved by long and patient research. Hence it is possible that any effort, even though inspired by genius, may prove disappointing.

Let us take Abner for an example. I discovered him about twenty years ago. Brought up in the wilderness, he was one of nature's favored sons. Logger, teamster, river driver, hunter, trapper, guide, and cook, he was past master of anything to which he turned his hand. I fell in love with his biscuits at my first taste. Fluffy as cotton balls, crispy but delicately browned on top, no other biscuits would ever seem the same after partaking of one of Abner's creations. The resulting friendship has lasted through the years, and Abner has presided over many a campfire for me since that time.

Artist that he is, one would naturally suppose that Abner would now be content to rest on his laurels, and confine his activities to serving those wonderful creations that have won him fame, but such is not the case. He will go along steadily enough for a while, and then the light of genius will kindle in his eye. From then until the idea is either perfected or discarded, one eats Abner's cooking at his peril, for even he does not know to what lengths he may go to achieve his purpose.

We had gone into the hills of western Maine: four hunters, a pack of fox dogs, and Abner to do the cooking. For the first week he outdid himself. Each meal was a triumph. Two of our quartet were quite overwhelmed, and one went so far as to suggest that we should apply for a congressional medal for Abner for outstanding achievement in the field of culinary art.

Then one night when we came tramping in after dark, I saw him standing in the center of the room regarding the hot stove contemplatively, and I could see the light of inspiration burning in his eye. On the cookstove a huge frypan sat, smoking hot and redolent of bacon fat. The larder consisted, in part, of a case of eggs, a bushel of potatoes, the loins of several rabbits, and the breasts of a brace of grouse in the icebox, plus several well-laden shelves of canned goods, but Abner would have none of these. He was in the throes of one of his creative moments, and I awaited the outcome with bated breath.

His roving glance swept the shelf where the canned goods were and centered on a large can of tomato soup. He regarded it gravely for a few moments, turning it slowly in his hand, then opened it and poured it into the sizzling frypan, stepped back and regarded it with the eye of a gourmet. A dog lying near the stove stood up and sniffed interrogatively, then, with its tail between its legs, crossed the room and lay down in the farthest corner. In rapid succession then, Abner added two cans of corn, a slab of smoked halibut, and a dash of anchovy sauce. Two more dogs got up and moved hastily from the vicinity of the stove.

A lesser man would have quit then, but Abner was fired with the same indomitable will that characterized General Grant. One by one, in order named, he stirred in half a dozen eggs, a double handful of corn meal, some cracker crumbs, two cans of condensed milk and a bottle of olives.

Another dog, a female and expectant mother, crawled over to the door and whined piteously to be let outside. I opened it and was almost overwhelmed in the general exodus, and when it was over only Ring remained. A hardy dog was Ring, but he was destined to meet his match.

The steam billowed and whirled, searching out every nook and corner. Ring stirred restlessly and a leg twitched convulsively. Then he got slowly to his feet; his gaunt stomach contracted with a sinuous, rippling movement that seemed to extend upward to his throat. The movement was repeated after a moment and seemed to even increase in intensity. It was evident that nature was about to take its course, and Ring was aware of it. He lurched to his feet, shot one reproachful glance at Abner and bolted through the open door.

Not always by any means, but sometimes, men are not the best cooks in the world.

The Secret of Parlin Lake

THERE WAS A MUTTER of thunder in the west, a hollow rumbling sound as though a pair of monstrous dogs were quarreling over a monstrous bone, while in the deepening dark lightning flashed behind the inky storm rack for a moment and was gone. The evil spirits that ruled the upper Kennebec Valley were assembling their forces for another assault on the trespassing white man, just as they had assembled them against Benedict Arnold two hundred years before.

On the long porch a match flared, startlingly bright in the Stygian gloom, and outlining the Old-Timer's rugged face as he applied the match to his guttering pipe.

"This starts out like the shower we had the day my father and

I learned the secret of Parlin Lake," he said, in that Down East accent that is no longer heard except in the deep woods of northern Maine. "You may have heard of my father. No? There are not many left who have. His name was Thompson. One of the best fisherman that ever lived. Owned the Pond Hotel for years until the Depression wiped him out. He's long gone now but he left me memories of fishing trips that I'll never forget, for I was his fishing companion and oarsman for a number of summers while I was growing up.

"My dates I don't recall too well, but I know it was during Prohibition days, for I remember going to the line house above Jackman to get a bottle of beer for a man stopping at the Parlin Lake Hotel. My Dad and I fished Parlin with three flies in those days: Palma Belle, Brown Hackle, and Black Gnat. I rowed him around the lake, and at times we both cast to shore. We picked up two small trout and were quite disappointed with the fishing. However, at the south end of the lake there is a big springhole which just at dusk can be seen quite clearly. We discovered this while watching a doe and two fawns walking on the sandy beach. An old gentleman came along the road and we pointed the deer out to him. This was how we learned the secret of Parlin Lake, a secret that you'd better see while you are here.

"The old gentleman proved to be Mister Piel of brewery fame. His house was just across from the springhole, and he told us this story. 'Fellows,' he said, 'if you want to see the biggest squaretail trout you ever hope to see in all your life, just come down to this springhole in a thunder storm, and you will see trout jumping like crazy all over the top of the springhole.' Like all kids, I thought he was telling us a fish story. However, it proved to be no story, as you will see.

"The following day we crossed Parlin and went in to Lang

Pond. It is—or was at that time—full of one- to two-pound trout. My Dad took a party farther in to Indian Pond, and I fished a little pond at the end of Lang on an old wood raft. Late in the afternoon I heard a woman scream. My blood ran cold. I looked up on a rock cliff over my head and saw the first and only mountain lion I have ever seen—or ever hope to see—that close to me. I'd seen bobcats and Canadian lynx, but when I saw a long tail hanging down I headed for shore on the other side of the pond, ran through the swamp to my boat, and down the pond to camp.

"When my Dad returned I was in favor of turning back to Parlin the following morning—I picked up a thirty-thirty and got out ahead of my father's party in a rainstorm. Before I hit Parlin it began to thunder, and lightning was running the telephone wire which went to Lang Camp. This flashing kept me on the trail to the shore of Parlin Lake. I think I made that trip faster than anyone ever will again. Knowing that Dad and his party were following me, I took the canoe to cross the lake and left the boat for him and the others.

"Needless for me to say, the wind was blowing a gale and it was rough. I got down on the floor of the canoe on one leg, and headed for the other shore. The wind hit me and drove me to the foot of the lake. It was a wicked thunderstorm, but as I crossed the springhole I saw squaretail trout splashing on top of he waves, and in spite of the fact that the canoe was half full of water, I stopped paddling to watch. I have never seen such a sight in all my life. The old man had been telling no fish story after all. I headed in and landed, pulled the canoe up on the beach, and headed for the hotel. Soon my Dad landed his party of city folks, who were scared to death. It was a good thing my Dad was there to row them across the lake, for he was a good oarsman.

"The lightning hit the telephone at the hotel and knocked me out, and when I came to I told my Dad what I had seen at the foot of the lake. He said, 'Get the boat while I get my rod.'

"I was too shaken up by the lightning, and told him to get one of the guides from the Forks, and he got a Mister Durgin. He told my father he couldn't swim, and my Dad said, 'If we go overboard I'll bring you ashore.' He was a good swimmer, but I don't think my Dad had anything on his mind at the moment but those squaretails.

"They took off for the springhole in the storm. Thunder and lightning as I have never seen. The wind all this time was blowing down the lake. My Dad held his Leonard rod high in the air. The wind was jumping those three flies across the waves, and as they hit the springhole a squaretail struck. Mr. Durgin held the boat as best he could while my Dad landed the fish. He took six squaretails, all over five pounds, and, as I recall, the largest was eight pounds. I am not sure of the exact weight, but those fish were given by my Dad to a gentleman at the hotel who wanted to have them mounted for the office of the Boston and Maine Railroad. As far as I know they are still with the Boston and Maine. I had a picture of those fish taken the next day. I remember that they were nailed to the top railing of the porch and their tails hit the porch floor. We don't get squaretails like those any more. I don't even know if the springhole is still there. Fishermen are not what they used to be either. Nine o'clock in the morning is as early as they'll get out, and they want to come ashore at the first sprinkle of rain."

It thundered again, ominously, a reverberation that seemed to emanate from mountains that were being rocked on their bases by malevolent spirits from a nether world. Lightning flashed again, closer at hand, and accompanied by a crackling sound not unlike the simultaneous breaking of a bundle of dry sticks. I could feel the movement as the Old-Timer drew back a trifle deeper into the recesses of the porch, while he relived for a time the happenings of a half century ago.

"If this storm shapes into what you would call a real one," a disembodied voice asked from the farther end of the porch, "what's the chance of having you take Bill and me down to the springhole about daylight tomorrow morning?"

"If it shapes into a real one," the Old-Timer answered, and I could detect dry humor in his voice "if it shapes up like that one, there won't be any daylight. And I don't fish during thunder showers any more. I might not be so lucky another time."

Incident at Middlebranch

I HAVE SEEN MORE elaborate fishing camps, and here and there I have seen others which were infinitely worse, but none of them has lingered more vividly in my mind than the one that John and George and I pitched close by the shore of an innocuous little pond in southern Maine one summer afternoon in the year of 1904.

We were each newly turned eighteen, with high school forever behind us—and the great wide world before us. Now, recognizing the broadening influence of travel, we were starting out on a horse-drawn safari on a roundabout course that would take us at one point a daring full thirty miles from home. Let it be said that in that year a horse-drawn vehicle of any kind was well out in the boondocks when it was that far from its native heath, and the distance seems infinitely greater at dusk, just after the first star has made its appearance and the wind is stilled.

Into that witching hour a stranger came, a furtive little man with bulging, lidless eyes which he used only when he stole surreptitious glances at our outfit.

"Paoutin'?" he asked, conserving his speech after the manner of Maine men, yet letting just enough seep through so that we could translate it into the query "Are you going to fish for hornpouts?"

I replied that the spiny bullheads were not on our agenda, and that this was but a stopping place on our trek to the Ossipees in a quest for brook trout.

"You plannin' to stay here overnight?" he asked, rolling his eyes at each of us in turn, and letting them finally come to rest on me and remain there in their unblinking stare.

"Why not?" I demanded, resenting his question for some unknown reason. "Why shouldn't we stay here? You own it, or something?"

"No," he said. "No. It ain't my propity. I thought I'd just drop in and warn ye."

"Warn us?" I asked. "About what?"

Again he favored us all with that dead-fish stare. "Didn't you ever hear about the Hawkins murder?"

I remembered it then, and very well indeed, for it had been Maine's chief subject of conjecture only a few years previously. As I recalled it, a crew of loggers had come in to strip the stand of pine that rimmed the pond. It was a combined operation by two parties, and trouble had arisen over property lines. The quarrel increased in intensity until someone, presumably Hawkins' enemy, settled the dispute by bashing in his opponent's head with an ax.

His vindictiveness was so great that, maddened by the blood bath, as he was, but still unsatiated, he attacked the two horses that were stalled in the nearby hovel, killing one outright and wounding the other so grievously that its screams were heard a mile away. Not until that moment did it dawn on my consciousness that the spot on which we had pitched our tent was the identical site where the lumberman's hut had stood, and that the horse hovel out there alone in the gathering dusk was the one from which the frenzied animals had broken away from the blood-maddened fiend, only a few years previously. Tradition had it that on certain moonless nights in early summer more than one inebriated traveler, passing the spot at midnight, had heard the hair-raising death cry of the stricken horse.

Ghost stories, as a general rule, never have disturbed me too greatly; in fact I rather like a good one that begins with the striking of a clock at midnight, and the first shuffling footstep on the attic stairs. The effect is greater when one is only eighteen. I recall that George, who had smuggled a 12-gauge shotgun into the load among our bedding, had dug it out and opened and closed the breech before leaning it conveniently against a potato sack.

We lit our second lantern before it was really needed, which marked any Maine man a profligate in the year 1904. I can recall, too, that all three of us went together to give the horse his hay and his full quota of grain, and that John, whose father was a sailor of sorts, objected to the way I had tied the halter rope, insisting that any horse that was clever with his teeth, as some of them were, could untie it, and that nothing but a bowline would do, for while a horse would be completely baffled by the bow-line's many twists and turns, the knot could be easily untied by anyone who possessed even a modicum of brains, which disqualified me.

The door was held closed by a light hasp and staple which kept it from swinging in a wind but offered little resistance to a horse that wished to break out of confinement; so to overcome that weakness, we upended an eight-foot log and braced it rigidly against the door. Houdini at his best could never have won his way outside.

"That'll hold him," John predicted, as he finished tying the bowline, and we went back to the tent.

I don't know what time it was, but I had the impression that it was about midnight when we were brought to our feet by a scream so appalling that it must have originated in the lower depths of Hades. Only once—from a horse trapped in a burning stable—have I heard anything that approached it in its lost-soul wail. I could feel the hair rise on my head, and I remember that the last chilling note had hardly died away before I heard the double click as George cocked both barrels of the shotgun. It augured ill for anything, either man or beast, to put his head inside the tent flap at that moment.

We were drawing our first long breaths when there came the sound of a heavy creature moving about in the lush grass around the tent. I fumbled in my pocket for a card of matches, but only John's fingers were steady enough to apply one to a lantern wick. I could hear George's teeth clicking like castanets—or perhaps they were mine. I'm not positive about that, but they very well could have been mine.

132

It is with considerable pride that I record the fact that we went outside. It is true that we emerged in a compact wedge or triangle, with George and the shotgun at the apex of the V, but we went out—a fact which, in my book, is the only thing that mattered. If we were about to die, we preferred to do so in the open.

The horse—for the frightening creature of the night proved to be only our stolid old farmhorse, Dick—was grazing a few yards from the tent. The heavy log which we had used to brace the door, lay ten feet away at one side. The leather halter, a sturdy affair, was properly buckled, but the halter rope—with its untied bowline—was dragging beneath the horse's feet. There were no other clues.

Well, that's the story, told just as it happened, too. I have pondered it frequently, sometimes in the revealing stillness of the night, but I have come to no rational conclusion. It seems to me that human hands must have been needed to move the log away from the door. I have barred the supposition that the scream was made by a screech owl, for no bird was ever hatched that could produce that volume of sound. Some have suggested that it was the wall-eyed native who engineered it all, but they have no suggestions as to why he did it. No profit would accrue to him if we were driven out. Furthermore, anyone found prowling around an occupied tent at midnight, particularly a tent where George guarded the entrance with a shotgun whose twin barrels were both loaded and cocked, stood a very definite chance of requiring the services of a tweezer-equipped medico in the immediate future.

So there the matter rests, in the limbo of almost forgotten things, and there I shall now let them lie.

Backyard Trout

"Tomorrow," I said, as I kicked the cat down the cellar stairs and reached for the clock key, "marks the first day of spring, Can you imagine it?"

My wife regarded me with some anxiety. "Have you gone completely cuckoo?" she asked. "Spring began six weeks ago."

"Not by my calendar," I assured her. "Spring begins the first day of open season on trout. That's tomorrow."

"Good heavens!" she exclaimed. "Just when I was beginning to feel the least bit acquainted with you. Now I suppose I won't see any more of you until July."

134

"August," I corrected her. "I'll look you up sometime after August 15."

"Where are you going—and when do you start?"

I drew off my slippers and began undoing my tie. "As a matter of fact," I told her, "I can't get away for at least a week, and I'll have to work like the devil to make it in that time."

Just then the doorbell rang. I slipped into my bathrobe and answered it. It was my neighbor, Jonesie, and he seemed excited.

"What's the matter?" I asked, as I drew him into the hall. "Somebody sick? The baby—"

"No," he said. "Everybody's all right, but I just got a telegram. They've been rising all day on the big river. Let's go up there."

"I can't," I said. "Not for a week anyway. I'm too busy."

"Just for a day," he pleaded. "You can spare one day."

"It's too cold," I countered. "And it's too far up there. We would miss the morning fishing."

"It will be warmer tomorrow; the radio said so. 'Fair and warmer.' We could start now and be on the river by daylight."

"What? Start now? At eleven? Ride all night, fish all day and then ride home again? No, thank you. I'm through doing stunts like that."

Jonesie sighed regretfully. "I suppose you are right," he said. "When a fellow gets to be your age he has to be careful."

"My age? What do you mean, my age? I'm a year younger than you."

"In years, perhaps. I was thinking of your physical condition."

"There's nothing wrong with my physical condition," I yelled at him. "It is too early to fish the big river. We could take more trout, and better trout, right here around town than we could up there at this time of year."

"Always fishing in your own doorway," he accused me. "If you want to take trout you have to go where they are."

"Yes," I agreed. "And you also have to go when they are rising. It's too early. There's still a lot of snow up there. I'm too busy. I'm not going."

The rascal grinned. "I was thinking about the big one you lost up there last spring. In the pool below the falls. You remember? I thought perhaps you might like to tie into him again before someone else did. Boy, was that a battle! My heart turned completely over when he went down through the rips. Well, I'm sorry you can't make it, but I think I'll go just the same. I'd sure like to fight it out with that baby. I'd show him who was the boss."

"Look," I said. "Maybe you could handle him better than I did, and maybe you couldn't, but if you get the chance to try it you'll have to lay a better fly than I can. Go home and get your car and tackle. In twenty minutes I'll be ready to go up there and give you a fishing lesson."

The eastern sky was only faintly pink when we parked the car in a gravel pit near the lower falls. The headlights played on some empty tar barrels and they looked suspiciously white. I stepped out of the car to investigate, and the air cut like a knife. As I had suspected, there was a quarter inch of frost on the barrels. I got back into the car where I could shiver more comfortably while I razzed Jonesie.

"Yah!" I jeered. "Fair and warmer, eh? I'll bet you forgot to bring an ice chisel."

136

"It'll warm up," he promised. "As soon as the sun gets up it will be all right. Let's take a nap."

Sleep, I knew, was impossible, but I thought it would be a good plan to rest my eyes for a few minutes—and when I opened them again, the sun was shining, the car windows were white with rime, and my legs were numb and lifeless.

"Come on," I yelled to Jonesie, and shook him savagely. "Let's get out of here before we freeze to death."

Hastily we assembled our rods and drew on our waders, our teeth chattering and our fingers all thumbs as we fumbled with our fly books. As we climbed down the embankment to the pool the grass crunched crisply underfoot. We paused at last on the twenty-foot ledge and peered down into the turbulent water. Then Jonesie pointed with a trembling forefinger and I looked in the direction it indicated.

It was a bit downstream from where we stood, an elongated, seemingly quiet place in the rushing water, and beneath it the gravel bottom of the pool would have been plainly visible had it not been for the fact that at least fifty—I swear it!—trout obscured it from our startled gaze. I could feel my pulse accelerate, and was aware of a sudden and pleasing warmth. The trout were lying in about ten feet of water, but despite the dwarfing effect they looked big.

"Jonesie," I said, "this is the day when we justify our existence. I'm going to put a curve in this rod that a chiropractor couldn't straighten with a ten-pound hammer."

An hour later I began to wonder if I had not, perhaps, spoken too hastily. Two hours later I had come to the conclusion that it would have been better if I had refrained from speaking at all. An hour after that I began to feel that the proper time for saying something pertinent to the occasion was rapidly approaching. I began arranging words and phrases, but before I had them grouped to my liking Jonesie beat me to it. He must have been dwelling on it for hours, for he rose to sublime heights. The trout endured it for a few moments, shrinking together at each withering blast, then dashed upstream as a single unit.

"There, dash blank 'em!" he said. "They've gone and I'm glad of it. I've offered them every fly in the book and not a dadburned one of them would so much as look at it."

It occurred to me to say, "I told you so," but I had the impression that to do so would be invoking an unnecessary risk. Presently I saw him glumly untying his leader. Silently I did likewise, reeled in the line, and unjointed the rod. Then, side by side, as mournfully silent as though we were a part of a funeral cortege, we walked back to the car.

Within a mile of my home the road runs for a few rods close beside a brook which once was excellent trout water. Where it turns to pursue its wandering way through heavy woods, an excellent pool has formed. The upper end is shallow enough to wade, but the lower half is satisfyingly deep, while an old pine on the bank affords it perfect shade. Many a time I have slipped out there for an hour just after sunset and taken a trout or two from under the abrupt bank. Native brook trout, they were, plump and firm, and red-fleshed as only native trout can be.

As we wheeled past it my eye swept the surface of the pool. It was only a momentary glance, but in the shadow cast by the old pine I saw a slight disturbance on the water, and around it a ring suddenly formed and slowly spread. I opened my mouth to speak, then closed it as an idea began taking shape in my mind.

When he left me in my driveway Jonesie said, "Well, this has

just been another one of those days, but we've at least inhaled a lot of fresh air. There's one thing certain, though. If you get 'em you have to go after 'em. You can't catch 'em by fishing in your own backyard."

I waited until he was out of sight, then unlocked the garage, stowed my equipment in the car, and drove out to the pool. The sun had set, and under the pine the water looked dark and mysterious. Even while I was tying on a small streamer a trout broke in the shadows.

Wading out in the shallow end of the pool, I worked out line and flipped the fly toward the deeper water. My cast was purposely short, for I wanted to fish the nearer part first, in hope that at least one trout would be cruising the shallows.

I had retrieved scarcely a yard of line when I saw that welcome, silvery flash, and as I flipped the rod tip upward I felt the hook slide home. Stripping in a few yards of line, I forced him to fight in the shallows, playing him as gently as possible in order to keep the disturbance down to a minimum.

Two minutes later I slid the net under him and was pleasantly surprised to find that he was larger than I had thought. The rule showed him to be eleven inches, and the blood-red spots along his sides proclaimed him to be a native, a survivor of that rapidly diminishing clan of river trout that formerly ran the brook from the time of the first spring freshets until the spawning season had ended in the fall.

Slipping him into the creel, I once more laid the fly along the edge of the deeper water. The cast was unrewarded, but on the next one I had a smashing rise. Once more we fought it out in the shallow water, and even while we were doing so I saw a fish break in the center of the pool, and heard a hearty splash from the deep shadows under the pine.

They're growing bigger and better, I thought, as I laid the rule on this one and found it lacked but a hair of being a full foot in length.

Again a fish rose, well out toward the center of the pool, but I drew him in with another purposely short cast. A smaller fish than the others, or so I judge, and the rule proved my guess to be correct. Only ten inches, but as I slid him into the basket I could feel it assume a bit of weight.

Carefully I covered all the nearer water, then lengthened line and laid the fly well out in the center of the pool.

Wham! When I set the hook in this one I knew I was fast to a fish. I invited him to come up in the shallows where we could fight it out man to man, but he was opposed to the idea. It was evident that he regarded that hole under the bank as Home Sweet Home, and he had a nostalgic longing to return to it, but I vetoed that proposition.

Back and forth across the pool he went; now fighting deeply in an effort to regain his coveted sanctuary, now threshing the water to foam as he splashed on the surface. Tiring at last, he permitted me to lead him into the knee-deep water, and a minute later he came to net. My twelve-inch rule was far too short to determine his length, but I noticed that when I laid him in my fifteen-inch basket his nose and tail touched the willow. With the addition of this one to the creel, the strap began to sag comfortably upon my shoulder.

As I once more whipped the fly across the pool I noticed that the shadows were deepening perceptibly. Under the high bank it was no longer possible to see the fly; consequently I missed a good rise, but hooked him on the next cast. This time he fought it out in the deep water. If the commotion the big fellow made had not disturbed them, it seemed unlikely that this one would seriously alarm any that might remain in the pool.

The figures on the rule were not deeply etched, but I thought the length of this one to be ten inches. When he was stowed away I hesitated and stole a glance at the sky. In the west a thin crescent of moon hung precariously, while in the east I caught the faint twinkle of the first star. It was time to quit, but the urge to make one more cast was too strong to resist. I worked out line and shot it toward the towering bank.

Even through the thickening dark I could see the creamy foam when his broad tail lashed the water, and I struck in anticipation of the forthcoming tug. It did not materialize, and reluctantly I began stripping in line.

Then he hit it. *Zowie!* What a smash. I wonder why it is that darkness causes one's imagination to run riot. Reason told me that this fish was no larger than the big one in the basket, but I found it hard to believe. Its dashes seemed stronger, and the pull on my wrist greater. Even the possibility that I might lose him became magnified in my mind until it assumed the proportion of a major calamity.

After minutes that seemed interminable, I worked him into the shallow and at last I had him in the net. The creel was a trifle narrower at the top and it was necessary to bend the fish into a bow in order to close the cover.

Back home once more, I went down to the basement and laid the beauties out on the cold cement in a straight line, the tail of one just touching the nose of another. Then I unfolded a six-foot rule and placed it beside them. The six fish measured 71 inches, an average of approximately 11¾ inches each.

I gloried over them for a few minutes, then replaced them in the creel, slung it over my shoulder, and went down to Jonesie's house. Through the window I could see that he was about to retire. Even as I looked he snapped a half-consumed cigarette into the fireplace, yawned, and got stiffly to his feet.

As I hooked the creel strap over the doorknob, I thought, *Jonesie is a mighty good fisherman and a mighty good friend. If he were not, I'd never risk doing what I'm going to do now.*

With that, I gave the bell a vicious jab, heard it shatter the silence within, saw Jonesie straighten and turn toward the door, and then I fled down the steps and into the concealing darkness of the night.

III / Quebec

Hard-Luck Trout

MOST OF US, I suppose, cherish some visionary dream spot, some Mecca that we must reach before dissolution sets in, and mine is the upper falls on the Manouan River in Quebec. To reach them one must ascend the Peribonka—the *Grand Peribonka*—some sixty miles, then branch off into the Manouan, and pole up for thirty-five miles more. Here is a series of falls, the last of which is too high for fish to leap, and in the pools below the falls is reported to be the best landlocked-salmon fishing in the world.

When I awakened from my own particular dream I immediately sent a telegram to our old outfitters at Pointe-Bleue. "Arrange two weeks' trip to Manouan Falls for June seventh." Then

I went over and told Ernie what I had done. Ernie is a shrewd businessman, and much of his shrewdness is due to the fact that he refuses to let business interfere too seriously with his fishing.

"Sure, I'll go," he said. Pushing the papers off his desk, he opened a drawer and dumped out three or four well-fitted fly books and immediately began taking a census of the contents.

Although they always drag interminably I like the happy anticipation of the last few days before starting a trip, but now trouble began to literally loom on the horizon. It had been an excessively dry spring, and local fires were keeping the wardens busy. Then the newspapers reported a huge blaze raging in the Saguenay region in Quebec. Tourists and fishermen were barred from entering the area, the papers unfeelingly informed us.

The Saguenay was far from the area we proposed covering, but nevertheless the report was disquieting. Unless it rained soon all forest travel would be banned. We could postpone the trip, but spring comes with a rush north of the Laurentians, and I like best to be there shortly after the ice goes out. The fish seem hungrier then, while the cool water gives them added stamina in a fight.

No rain fell, but when the day of our scheduled departure came we argued that inasmuch as we had received no telegram to the contrary, conditions must be at least possible, so we bundled our dunnage into the car and started out.

We were nearing the border, and the hour was nearing midnight when the blow fell. The entire Peribonka country, the radio informed us, was wrapped in the province's worst conflagration. Forest travel was banned in that area also and might be extended in a few hours to include the rest of the province.

I know of no optimism so great as that which perennially

blooms in the heart of a fisherman. Our hesitation was only a momentary one, and then I bore down harder on the accelerator. There would be an isolated stream somewhere where we could fish, and once we were there the fire could do whatever it chose. If it came our way we could submerge and wait it out. Of such stuff are fishermen made.

Then another blow fell. The radio now informed us that the road to Chicoutimi was also barred to travel. Our only hope now was that the road through the park would remain open. Some men would have quit then, but not us. By some magic which has never become entirely clear to me—a magic which involved storming the Park Commissioner's home at three o'clock in the morning, plus the kindly intervention of a Catholic priest and a fish and game official, we emerged with a special permit to go in over the Laurentide trail.

As we topped the mountain range and swung downward at last into the Lake St. John Valley a vague yellowness began to encompass the world. Horizons narrowed, the hills behind us became vague and indistinct, while the sun hung like a huge copper ball in the leaden sky. Somewhere ahead of us in the lush forest that stretched from Dolbeau to Hudson Bay, hundreds of square miles were wrapped in seething flame.

We could now both see and smell the smoke, and for the first time I began to doubt the wisdom we had displayed in pushing on after that first warning. Could we get into the bush far enough to find good fishing?

I knew from experience that the miles were interminable in that vast country, and many of them were won only at the expense of grievous toil, and now we might find the toil and the hazards greatly increased.

At four that afternoon we pulled into Pointe-Bleue, and Tommy Robertson came out with both arms stretched aloft in a gesture of utter dismay. "I send telegram," he explained. "You get him, no?"

I said, "No. It must have come after we left."

He shrugged helplessly. "Very bad," he said. "Very bad. Bush closed, road closed, river closed, Big fire. You stay here and fish lake for ouananiche?"

Under ordinary circumstances there are few things I like better than fishing for landlocked salmon in most of Quebec's waters, but now a cyclonic wind was sweeping down the thirty-mile expanse of the lake, and whitecaps were doing their mad dance as far as the eye could reach. Tommy, always the perfect host, asked again, solicitously, "You stay here and fish?"

"We'll stay here and pray," I told him. "We'll stay here and pray for rain."

For three days the wind blew without a trace of letup, while with each passing hour the smoke thickened, and the tang of buring spruce came sharply to our nostrils. We wandered through the Indian village, or sat for hours in a sheltered niche on the rocky shore, morosely watching the storm-tossed water and wondering when the wind would cease and the fires be brought under control. I know of no penalty so severe, no judgment so harsh, as the one that permits a fisherman to approach the very gates of Paradise and then bars him from entering.

We fretted and fumed, and cursed the careless individuals who were responsible for the fire, but still the wind howled, and the smoke pall grew nearer and more opaque. Then all at once hope surged anew.

The west wind veered abruptly into the south, the amber skies assumed a brighter hue. Thunder rolled in the distance, and a rain squall swept up across the lake. In another hour the sun was shining fitfully once more, but far to the west we could see the vertical gray lines which indicated that another rain squall was passing there.

We went back to headquarters and spent the rest of the day frantically telephoning everybody in Quebec who had the slightest influence with the Department of Lands and Forest. They were adamant though, insisting that, compared to the Peribonka holocaust, Hades was merely a sputtering campfire. Reluctantly we consigned the Peribonka trip to the limbo of forgotten things, and centered our attack on the Lake Claire region.

A minor conflagration had raged there: a baby fire only thirty miles long and fifteen miles wide, but now it was practically under control. Could we go in there? At first they said "No," but our passionate pleadings wore them down and they half-heartedly agreed that inasmuch as the fire had consumed every inflammable thing in the area, and that it would be a hundred years before it could possibly burn again, they reluctantly issued us a *permis de circulation en forest* in the district of *Branche Oriente*.

"Wonderful!" we cried gleefully, and began planning the trip. Our permits authorized us to *circulate on the forest*, so circulate we would. We would strike up through Salmon River and Lake Clair and then swing south in the beginning of a great half-circle through Big and Little Beaver lakes to Lake St. Croix. Using that lake as a base, we would fish several neighboring ponds, then swing down through Otter and Island lakes to Rabbit Lake. Short portages here would take us in to Bear and Spruce lakes for a try at old *Cristovomer namaycush*, the big lake trout of the north, and thence down Rabbit River to our rendezvous with the truck.

Grateful that we were at last beginning to get the breaks, we

helped load the canoes on the cars and started off through St. Félicien and Notre-Dame-de-la-Dore to a nightmarish road that brought us, some four hours and forty miles later, to Salmon River. And now I'll let my diary pick up that tale.

"Tuesday, June 10. So this is Salmon River. I wonder when it was named. It doesn't look like salmon water to me. Too flat, and the current is sluggish. I must ask Willie about it. Willie Larouche is Ernie's guide—French and Indian, I should surmise. My guide is Kenneth Moore. Young chap, soft-spoken and knows some English, but has a lot of Montagnais blood in him, or I'm no anthropologist. Asked Willie, and he said, 'No salmon.' Oh well, there has to be a Salmon River somewhere.

"Had dinner on shore, then went on. Only one portage between us and Lake Clair, but it is a hard one, Kenneth said. It was. Reached Lake Clair in midafternoon. A nice little lake about two miles long and a half mile wide, narrowing like an hourglass in the middle. Took a dozen or more trout while we were cruising for a camping spot. Had trout for supper and, oh boy! They are the genuine, unadulterated natives with meat as red as canned salmon.

"Went out on the lake after supper and had some fine fishing. Thirteen trout over a foot in length. Among them was a two-pounder and one of two and a half pounds. Tonight they seem to like best a streamer of guinea-hen feathers tied on a bright green body. Trout are queer fish. I doubt if they will look at that fly tomorrow.

"Thousands upon thousands of them were schooling on the main lake just before dusk. Can't remember that I have ever seen them do that in such quantities before. They traveled like schools of white perch, their back fins just out of water, but a fly would put them down. As usual, our best fishing was just at sunset, when the trout began to come in to shallow water to feed. A clear sky, but it was growing cold. Those Hudson's Bay blankets will be appreciated tonight.

"Wednesday, June 11. An extremely cold night kept us in bed later than we had planned, and the trout had stopped rising— if they did rise. However, after we had scraped the last crumb of those big trout from the frypan, we paddled up to a small stream which connects Lake Clair with Island Lake. It is a small fall and the most delightful pool one can imagine.

"Here we could take trout at every second or third cast. Several times we had doubles on. We caught and released twenty or more, then went on and circled Island Lake, hoping to raise a good fish, but no dice. Plenty of ten- and twelve-inchers, but there is no fun in that after last night. I am led to believe that trout of the same age keep more or less together. If this lake is similar to the others that I know up here, there will come a day when big trout will be rising and taking, too. I hope it will be to-morrow.

"Back to camp for dinner. Lay around until supper, then went out and took twenty-six ranging from nine to twelve inches. Released them all. I like big trout—on a fly rod or in a frypan—but the big ones were still not taking. Back to the camp, put a few more spruce tips on the bed, and it feels inviting.

"Thursday, June 12. Up with the birds this morning. Built fire for the guides, then went for a swim while they were preparing breakfast. Br-r-r! Broke camp and started for Lake St. Croix. Five portages on this day's trip, and one of them is a mile long. I wonder why we always pack so much stuff. Went through Big and Little Beaver lakes, but did not fish much, for we were in a hurry to get here. Kenneth, who carries the food pack, runs when he tires of walking, says it rests him. He may run with mine if he wants to.

"This is reputed to be a lake that contains some good brookies, and it looks promising. The water is deep and fairly clear, and the shores are rocky. Pitched camp, had an early supper and hurried out, for they were beginning to rise. We took about thirty nice ones—several better than two pounds, but still no big ones. Again we kept two for breakfast, and on opening them we found them stuffed with pond shiners. Why wouldn't it be a good idea to bring a trolling rig next time, get some live bait and go down to the bottom after some of those five-pounders?

"This has been a really worthwhile day. Our luck has certainly changed at last.

"Friday, June 13. Slept loglike all night. Up at five. Shaved and had breakfast. Ernie is down on the shore taking pound trout at almost every cast waiting for the guides to finish washing dishes. Day is overcast, threatening rain. Slight ripple on the lake and trout are rising everywhere. Should be a great day.

"Portaged in to Beaver Lake No. 2. Took about twenty trout. Kept the three best ones. One was sixteen and a half inches. Ernie's day today. I took the two smaller ones, and they gave me a good clean fight. A lot of vigor in these northern squaretails.

"This afternoon we portaged back to Lake Clair to try for trout in that crystal clear water. Found seven stranded firefighters who had been cut off and took refuge at the lake. They were hungry. The larder down to a little flour and a bucket of lemon pie filling. Proposed that we should fish and trade the catch for lemon pie. Did so and filled dishpan with beauties. Pie was no culinary triumph but we ate it. First time I ever fished commercially.

"This is a very pretty lake—or was until the fire swept the

shores. It is surprising how devastating a fire can be in virgin softwood. This one traveled fifteen miles in eight hours when at its height, sweeping along through the tree tops and burning off the green limbs. It left a forest of bare poles which are already beginning to fall in jackstraw confusion, for in many places the roots are burned completely off, together with the accumulation of centuries, to a depth of a foot or more. The moose trails, instead of being hollows, are now ridges, for they were packed too hard to burn. The startling thing is the completeness of it all. Not a living tree or shrub is left. Reforestation will be slow here.

"Saturday, June 14. Today promises to be fishless, for it is very foggy and threatens rain. Think we will go up the river to Otter Lake. Then, if it doesn't storm too hard, we'll have a try for the big ones. This may be the day. Ashore for lunch and to rest my weary arms. Has this been a wonderful morning! No rain yet, and the trout are rising everywhere. Released more than twenty fish weighing from one to two pounds. Took one that weighed a little over three pounds. He was nineteen inches long and five inches deep. A nice trout and he had a will of his own.

"Kenneth had dinner ready. The trout are still rising. Think perhaps I'd better get out after them right away. They might stop rising at any time. Dark Montreal was their favorite fly this morning. A healthy curse on those ankle-length waterproof shirts. Got tangled up in mine down on the shore and slipped on the wet boulders. I have either sprained or dislocated my right wrist, and writing is a torture. Thought at first it was broken, but Willie Laroche says no. I am keeping hot compresses on it, and Kenneth is hewing a splint which I will have to wear for a few days.

"My hand is swelling badly and turning a sort of greenish-purple. No more fly-fishing for me on this trip, but I certainly had more than my share today.

"Sunday, June 15. I could write better than this when I was five years old. My wrist is in a splint, my fingers are swollen so that I can't move them, and I'm the least left-handed man in the world. Managed to take some pictures of those two big trout, but am worried about the camera. Was wearing that when I fell, and I'm afraid it didn't do it any good. The case seems to be sprung. I hope it's all right. I sure want pictures of that biggest trout. Stayed in camp all day, keeping hot packs on my wrist. It feels somewhat better tonight. A glorious sunset. I love to watch a lake go to sleep.

"Monday, June 16. Went again to Otter Lake, hoping to pick up another big trout on a trolled fly, but a two-pounder was the best I could do. It was Ernie's day today. He took two three-pounders and five that averaged about two pounds each. Smaller trout (under a pound) were a nuisance today. They were rising everywhere on the lake. Have always wanted to learn to cast left-handed, but never could seem to waste the time when fishing. I tried it this afternoon and was surprised. Before quitting I could get out twenty feet of line. Not much accuracy, but it is better than trolling.

"A queer thing happened today. My wrist was, as the saying goes, giving me fits, but I was up there to fish, and a mere broken wrist was not going to stop me. I had Kenneth rig my trolling rod with a heavy line and a big streamer fly. Letting out fifty feet of line, I put the rod in the holder and went back to my left-handed fly-fishing.

"We had gone thus for a few minutes when a small trout took

my fly. I gave it slack line, thinking it might shake itself off and save me the trouble, and something that looked like a small whale came up and grappled it. Well, there I was with one thumb and two fingers with which to play a trout that would weigh five pounds if I ever saw one that did. Kenneth would have helped if I had permitted him to, but it was my fight, and would continue to be mine, win, lose, or draw.

"I like to think I did as much as any man could have done under the circumstances, but it was not enough. Once I had it almost near enough to the canoe for Kenneth to net, but that was the best I could do. Eventually the small fly worked loose, and that was that. I was sorry, for he would have fitted that place on the mantel that I have reserved for my first five-pound squaretail.

"Tuesday, June 17. We are leaving for Rabbit Lake—fourteen miles, seven portages. Stopping here at Island Lake for lunch. Three more portages ahead. Took several fair trout this morning. Am doing very well left-handed. Came through Rabbit Lake without raising a fish, but who cares? It has been wonderful fishing on all the other ponds and lakes. I have caught enough brook trout to feed a small army. Tomorrow morning we are going in over a short portage to Bear Lake, for another try at old Namaycush. The truck is supposed to meet us at noon to take us back to Pointe-Bleue. I'm tired and my wrist is still badly swollen and very lame.

"Wednesday, June 18. Went at six this morning by short portage to Bear Lake. Took a four-pound lake trout the first thing. Good fight. The fire spared this immediate section and the lake is very beautiful. Spruce intermingled with white birches line the shores, and the ground rises in gently rolling hills far to the northward. Went back to Spruce Lake and took two more lakers, both smaller than the first one. This was another morning when Ernie drew a blank. He's a far better fisherman than I, but somehow I seem to be luck's favorite child—if you don't count the wrist. Went by another short carry to Carcajou Lake. Took one sluggish fighter, and then back to camp and a trout dinner. Lakers are oilier than brook trout but not bad. They are preferred by the Indians.

"The truck is here. More later. What a road! Five hours doing seventy miles. In consideration of my wrist, was given seat beside driver. A mistake. Half the time I was in the driver's lap. Other half he in mine. It didn't do my wrist any good. Start home for X rays tomorrow.

"Well, that about wraps it up. X ray showed wrist broken in two places. Camera in same trouble. I'm all through fishing—until my wrist heals. The doctor says that will be at least two months. Just in time for fall fishing."

Barometric Pressure

WE WERE FISHING ALEX, and we were having a miserable time of it. Lake Alex is a trout lake, and as every trout fisherman knows, trout lakes are unpredictable. Like the little girl who when she was good was very, very good, but at other times was a little stinker, so our lake was playing hard to get.

Tommy Robertson, our outfitter, had a log cabin there for the convenience of his customers, and on the peeled logs were penciled little notes concerning the fishing: a 23-pound lake trout; a 5-pound squaretail; trout taken on a fly; and others taken on trolled lures.

But life, it seemed, was not all beer and skittles, even at Lake Alex. A disgruntled Midwesterner wrote: "After traveling a thousand miles to find good fishing, I can heartily recommend this lake for boating and swimming." After covering the lake from end to end several times we might have said the same thing, for we could not take half enough fish to eat. As for swimming, the water was still ice cold, and boating gets tiresome after a time, especially if one is sitting flat down on a canoe bottom. To tell the truth, we were getting fed up with Lake Alex. Why didn't it sparkle and ripple as a lake is suppose to do? Why didn't the sun break through the leaden clouds? Why didn't the wind blow and stir the fish into action?

It was seven o'clock that June afternoon when my prayer for a bit of wind was answered. It came from down the lake, in the east, and it came fitfully, in little squalls that writhed and twisted around us for a few moments before they went spiraling up the lake toward camp. Following it from far down the lake another squall materialized, and as it swirled about us I could sense a new power behind it when it slithered and squirmed past. I was aware that the sky had grown appreciably darker.

Then the fish struck in. Here and there on both sides of the border I have seen trout go on a wild feeding spree. Once in particular, in Cold River, which Maine and New Hampshire share jointly, I have, during a mayfly hatch at deep dusk, dipped trout in a small landing net from their station behind my legs, but I had never before seen action to compare with what we experienced that evening.

The Cold River trout were plentiful enough and were feeding voraciously, but they would accept only such flies as represented the naturals, but the Lake Alex fish would take anything. Wet flies, dry flies, nymphs, or streamers were all the same to them. If a fly moved they took it in an authoritative, no-nonsense way, and as far as we could see down the lake in the deepening gloom other legions had gone equally mad.

That the scene was primitive, I am well aware. I know that for my own part a frenzy had seized me, not to kill fish, but to shake the hook out and flip the fly out again before the action stopped.

All this time I had forgotten about the wind, but now I realized that those first gusts had increased fourfold. There was a menacing power in them that warned me it was time to go, and deepening gloom confirmed my judgment. Something told me that I should not have prayed quite so hard for rain. With a yell to Ernie to follow us, we headed for camp.

Then came the roaring sound of a giant exhaling a deep breath—and we were engulfed in a turmoil of shrieking wind and lashing rain that hurled us bodily toward the sandy shore and the sheltering log house.

Hastily we removed our fishing gear while the guides piled rocks and boulders inside the canoes to keep them from blowing away, which they surely would have done, for the wind steadily increased until the guides were hard pressed to move against it. Then the roof began to leak, following us from place to place and aiming with uncanny accuracy. Then the roof began to disintegrate. There was a four-foot porch built over the door, and the roof had been made by splitting five-foot logs and hollowing them out in a sort of elongated wooden tile. These the mighty wind seized, stood them on end, and then hurled them up the sloping roof to go bumping and thumping down the opposite side.

It was a long night, but the morning dawned rosy and bright, a promise of a beautiful fishing day. While the guides were straightening up the camp, Ernie and I assembled our rods and walked down the shore to pick up a few fish for breakfast, but we failed to get a rise. I do not know much about the effect of barometric pressure on fish. I have heard it said that they will not feed when the barometer is falling. This may be right, but I think if we had had a barometer along it surely would have registered something less than normal on that wild and memorable night.

The Long Trail

Accompanied by my Montagnais Indian guide, Tomo, I was trolling for salmon around one of the many points that stretch out into Lake St. John in the Indian reservation, when from the opposite side of the point and a short distance away I heard the sound of a shotgun blast.

There is something startling about the discharge of a firearm during the season of the year when hunting is prohibited, and a single shot is doubly so. All manner of thoughts flashed through my mind. Had some one chosen this moment to settle a grudge of long standing? Had an unhappy lover decided that life was no longer worth living? Or was it one of those accidents that occur with clocklike regularity whenever boys and guns get together?

I wondered about it as we rounded the point, and my interest was heightened when I saw two distant figures jump into a canoe and head out into the lake. The act in itself was not unusual, for it was seldom that one could not see a canoe somewhere along the shore, but the pair who drove this one were in a hurry. Their paddles flashed in perfect unison, and the stroke was unbelievably fast. At each shoulder surge the craft seemed to almost leap from the water, and white spray flew from its speeding prow.

Things were growing interesting. If these were murderers or robbers making their escape, why was not someone shooting at them from shore? On the other hand, if they were the attacked party, why didn't the would-be murderer seize this easy opportunity to pick them off before they got out of range?

I glanced back at Tomo, and asked him what it was all about, but he shook his head. He did not seem very much perturbed about the matter. Evidently it was not at all uncommon for his kinsmen to revert to first principles and remove from the landscape those of whom they disapproved.

Swiftly the two drove the canoe out into the lake, on a course that was bringing them nearer to us each moment. I could make out the occupants more clearly now—a big muscular fellow in the stern, a slighter and more graceful chap in the bow. They crossed in front of us, at a distance less than a hundred yards, and them I saw that the bow paddler was a woman.

An elopement! I thought, and had reason to believe so, for as the morning sunlight fell more fully upon the pair, I could see that they were not only young but also in a state of happy excitement. Evidently the old man had missed his aim, or else the gunshot was merely intended to hasten the pair to the priest. No need of that, I thought, for coming back to me in the bright sound of their voices was a note that was universal in any tongue. Wed or unwed, they were happily in love, and nothing else in the world mattered.

Straight out into the lake they drove, to where the wind that was no longer hampered by the shore stirred the waters until their crests ran white. Then, in the twinkling of an eye, the canoe abruptly changed its course, leaped ahead, spun around again and started toward us, while the girl, defying all laws of safety and gravity alike, stood in the bow, with paddle poised for an instant blow at something in the water.

Behind me, I heard Tomo's grunt, and I turned to him for an explanation.

"Shoot loon," he said. "Break wing, try for catch."

"Why don't they shoot again?" I asked.

"No more shell, maybe," he surmised, and swinging the canoe around where we could watch more comfortably, he laid his paddle across the thwarts and reached for his pipe.

"Not good for shoot loon," he said.

"No? Why not?"

"Make luck bad. No beaver find trap. No fox in snare. Much trouble come."

Strange how that old superstition went the rounds. I had encountered it in a half-dozen places along the Maine coast among coot shooters, but I had hardly expected to run across it here.

"You're an old woman, Tomo," I said, and settled back to watch such superb canoemanship as I had never before seen.

Among the divers, the loon is the peer. He can descend to tremendous depths. He uses his wings as an auxiliary to his feet, and his speed under the water is phenomenal. His ability to keep it up for hour after hour, with only momentary intervals when he pushes his bill above the surface for air, marks him as a bird with a physical stamina second to none, but this one needed every-thing that nature had given him, for two superb creatures were hot upon his trail and bent upon his destruction.

Never were two canoeists in more perfect accord, and never was rhythm and balance more perfectly executed. As the hunted creature neared the surface to expel the exhausted air from its lungs and draw in a new supply, they would drive down upon it like light, and in the midst of their flight the girl would stand erect in the dancing bow and try to drive the unfortunate crea-ture down again with a shrewd blow of the paddle before its breath could be renewed. Then, marking its new course, they would wheel the canoe cleanly around with a single sweep of their paddles, and dart off again in the new direction, laughing in all the exuberance of their youthful energy, yet moving as grimly and relentlessly as Fate.

Tomo filled his pipe, picked up his paddle, and would have moved on again, but I bade him wait. I was not particularly con-cerned with the outcome, but the poetry of their teamwork was something that was worth traveling far to see. We lay there for an hour, while the chase worked far out into the lake, where the hunted creature eventually eluded them and made its escape. They came in laughingly, waved merrily at us as they passed, and went in to where a new white tent stood half hidden among the trees. Tomo picked up his paddle, but as he swung the canoe around he said soberly:

"Not good to shoot loon."

That night I chanced to meet the Indian Agent, and I men-tioned the affair to him. He knew of it already, as he knew of everything that happened there. I had been right in at least a part of my guess. The youngsters had married when he came down from the trapline two weeks before.

"Will she go back with him this winter?" I asked.

He seemed surprised at the question.

"Of course," he said. "It is her place to go."

The next year I went to Nova Scotia, but the following spring I was back again on the reservation. We sat on the rude steps of the Agent's simple shack, listening to the lap of the waters on the graveled shore at our feet, and talking of many things. It was nearing the hour of twilight and the reservation was coming to life. The smoke of cooking fires drifted lazily with the wind, and out in the lake before us a half dozen canoeloads of children splashed and shouted riotously.

Presently, driving down through them, a lone voyageur came. Even in the distance I marked the easy manner in which he wielded his paddle, but as he neared us I could see that he moved listlessly, and that his shoulders were bowed as though he carried a great burden. Memory stirred within me and I turned to the agent.

"Isn't that the fellow who shot at the loon?" I asked.

"Yes," he said. "I think perhaps it was a mistake."

"Why?" I asked. "What happened?"

He crushed the fire in his cigarette and snapped the butt far out upon the shelving beach. Then, while the night closed down around us, he told me an unforgettable saga of two who went into the white wastes together.

It was mid-August (the Agent said) when Malec and Monique started north, and only two families of his tribe went before him. They were traveling far, and they needed to start early and move swiftly if they were to get in before the freeze-up, for the days were as short as the trail was long.

Malec and Monique had started early for similar reasons, for they too were traveling far. Malec had a general idea of the locality he was to trap, but he had not yet seen it. Custom demanded that now that he was the head of a family, he must seek a new base from which to operate his trapline.

The distance—as the Gold Company's red monoplane flew— was only four hundred miles, but when one travels by canoe in the north country it is seldom that distance may be measured thus. Your outfitter may tell you: "Twenty days it takes to Rupert River," for he knows that while the flashing paddles may set you thirty miles upon your way between sun and sun of one day, an equal amount of time and double the amount of labor will account for scarcely more than five on the day following.

So Malec started early, with Monique paddling in the bow, and all their worldly goods piled in the eight-foot space between them. The goods were not many, but they were enough. A tent, a sheet-iron stove that folded flat, and four Hudson's Bay blankets were all the insurance they carried against a temperature that might reach fifty below. There were a few beaver and muskrat traps, but Malec would depend chiefly upon his copper-wire snares for foxes and mink. The remainder of the canoe load was fuel, not for the flat stove, but for their own sturdy bodies, which would need it before the long arctic winter had ended.

Packed in four sealed tins was an even hundred pounds of lard. Now the moose were fat, but when the snow came they would rapidly grow so lean that a man could scarcely eat enough of their flesh to generate the body heat that he needed. When that day came, Monique would boil the meat and then drop it into simmering hot lard, until it once more dripped with life-giving fat.

There was a package of tea (a pound for every week they would be away), two one-hundred-pound sacks of flour, fifty pounds of sugar, and a few trifling things that had caught Monique's eye in the Company store. Curiously, although they would be gone for ten months, there was not so much as a spoonful of salt among their provisions, nor would they have used it had there been, for neither of them had tasted it, unless per chance they had eaten white man's food.

They were two days in reaching the mouth of the Mistassini, for they followed the curve of the great lake and kept close to shore. It was a mile across the river at its mouth, but it narrowed rapidly as they followed it upstream, and as it narrowed, so did its current increase. They paddled steadily and tirelessly, but it took them two more days to reach the first falls on the river, some forty miles from its mouth.

Now their work began, for the days that they had already spent were a mere preliminary to those which were to come. It required three trips to carry their provisions around the half mile of fast water, and they had paddled a scant five minutes before it was necessary to repeat the whole process. In that single group there were thirteen falls, which meant that all their equipment must be packed around them an equal number of times, but they did not complain. It was the way of their people, and they knew nothing else. They were happy, for they were together, and much of life lay before them.

The way was easier after they crossed the height of land, for now the streams ran toward the north, but it was nearing the end of September when at last they pitched their tent beyond the headwaters of the Rupert, and the ice was already beginning to form along the edges of the quiet ponds.

Malec killed a moose the next day, a two-year-old cow, and fleshed the hide carefully, for there would be need for snowshoe filling and moccasins ere the winter had ended. He scouted his trapline and laid out the course he would follow when the ice had closed the streams and made them safe for travel, and daily he found new causes for rejoicing. He had never seen beaver sign so plentiful. He had counted five of their conical huts along the shores of one small pond. Mink tracks were everywhere, and not a day passed that he did not see several of them, their coats were already showing the black of their winter richness. There were foxes, too, and martens in the spruce thickets, while of the little snow-white weasles there was no end. Malec was glad that they had sought the priest's blessing ere they left, for in addition to the security it gave them it could not fail to be a profitable sort of venture as well. He would show his appreciation to the good father when he sold his furs next summer.

Winter came, and with the first snows Malec started out, while Monique banked the tent high with the powdery stuff to shut out the cold winds. She dragged in wood and stacked it nearby, for there would be days when it would mean almost certain death to venture out after it through the whirling snow. She bent strips of pliant birch into bearpaw snowshoes and wove them with the tough moosehide, and from the thick leather along the back she made sturdy moccasins, crimping their toes with her strong young teeth and lacing them tight with thongs stretched until they were tough as wire.

By the last of November the snow lay five feet deep on a level, and more fell almost daily, thin, frosty particles that sifted endlessly down from a flat, gray sky; but as the snow increased, so did their treasure of furs also grow. It was Monique's task to care for them, fleshing them carefully, and drying them for a few days in the hot air at the top of the tent before she stacked them in the bales that grew and grew as week followed week, and month after month slipped away.

And now the sun rode higher in the sky, for February had ended and March was upon them. Winter still held them in its grip, but in another two months the ice would soften and go out, and they would take up the homeward trail. Malec's heart gladdened at the thought, but Monique's knew a depressing heaviness. An ordeal lay before her from which there was no escape, and she was beginning to be ridden by a nameless dread. The great white solitude that encompassed them seemed to be closing in around her, and for the first time she realized the magnitude of the thing that she must face.

Still she kept her counsel, going uncomplainingly about her tasks, but one night when the cry of a wolf awakened her she lay and listened to it—thinking how like the wailing of a lost soul it was. Then, all at once she knew that she was deathly afraid.

It was not good, Malec thought, that Monique should be left so much alone, but there was no way that he could help it. As the months had passed it had been necessary for him to extend his trapline farther and farther in order to continue to take furs. Mile by mile he had pushed it out, until now its farthest point was twenty miles away. It was not possible to cover it in a single day, and so he built a crude hut of spruce boughs and bark, and there he slept on alternate nights.

This was the life as they knew it, and neither complained, although each would have changed it had there been a way, for there was a loneliness about the great wastes that only human companionship could dispel. It was the great emptiness that Monique dreaded, for of the living dangers she had no fear. The bears had long since sought their winter dens, while the moose had always been harmless creatures. The wolves, too, had learned that man was master, and although they howled their protest against his invasion of their domain, they would slink carefully away whenever they caught the taint of his body.

But Monique was afraid and her fear was worse because it was not a fear of living things. Creatures of flesh and blood could be killed or driven away, but the great emptiness that was around them could not be repelled. Day by day as she went about her work, and night after night as she lay listening, she could feel the emptiness crowding in upon her, until she longed to cry out at it, or run, screaming, from the remorseless thing from which there was no escape.

Through it all Malec was kind, for there was kindness in his heart. "Today it is bad, but tomorrow will be better," he would tell her comfortingly, when he saw how quiet she was. Then, because of the goodness that was in him, he helped her flesh the skins he had brought, and drew wood from the forest that her burden might be lightened.

Each day the sun rose higher, and although winter still held them in its grip, there was a hint of spring in the air. When the sun shone brightly and the wind was stilled, he could feel the snow softening beneath his webs, and he was glad, for when the crusts came it would make traveling easier.

Then one night when he was in his hut at the end of the trail a storm broke. Driving out of the north it came, whooping, howling, shrieking, driving stinging snow pellets before it, and piling them in windrows and drifts of unbelievable height.

To venture out in it would be suicide, for it would have worn him down and beaten him to death before he had covered a mile of the journey, so he lay quietly and waited for the storm to blow itself out. He had no uneasiness about Monique. There was fuel enough for the stove, and no lack of food. Banked as it was with snow, the tent would be as warm as anyone could wish, and not to be compared to his own flimsy structure.

Had he been inexperienced or given to panic, Malec's own plight would have been serious, for it was impossible to build a fire and prepare food, but he lay quietly in his bunk, conserving his energy and body heat all the next day and far into the following night. Then, when the wind died, he arose and prepared for the battle that lay ahead. He brewed his tea doubly strong, and ate heavily of moose meat that he had cut into small pieces in order that it might absorb more fat. Then, when he could eat no more, he spread the blankets around his shoulders so that they would act as a reflector, and let his body drink in the heat from the fire. Then when it was light enough to see the way, he started back.

It was hard going until he reached the river, but here the wind had swept the snow down to the old trail and he made better time, but it was dusk before he reached the tent. As he came up, he noticed that no smoke was rising from the bit of stovepipe that protruded through the roof, and he knew a sudden, chill premonition of disaster. He went in hurriedly.

Monique was lying on her bed of boughs, and she was breathing with a labored, rasping effort. The fire had died long since, but she was not cold. Instead, she was burning with fever, and her body was moist beneath its blanket. She neither opened her eyes, nor showed by any sign that she was aware of his presence, yet something told him that she knew and was glad that he had come when he did.

174

He lighted the fire hurriedly, and set water on to heat, then rushed out and came back with an armful of moosewood tips. He boiled them in the kettle, and forced some of the liquor down her throat, then dipped cloths in it and applied them to her tortured body. Through the night he did what he could, but it was not enough, for she died just as dawn was breaking and she died without giving birth to her child.

When it was over, he sewed her in her blanket, and bound it tightly about her with thongs of moose hide. Then he carried the burden out into the forest, and after repeated failure managed to secure it firmly to the top of a bent spruce where no wandering forest creature could reach it.

For three days, then, Malec kept a lonely vigil within the tent, and during all that time he neither ate nor slept, but sat there, a broken man, alone in the eternal solitude. Then he took up his duties once more.

Spring came early that year, but it was the last week in May before the ice went out of the river. When it was free, Malec sorted his pelts carefully, made two small packs of the very finest, and lashed them securely in the bow and stern of the canoe. From the scanty store of provisions he chose only enough to sustain him on his journey, and leaving the rest to the squirrels and wood mice, he unlashed the burden from the treetops, laid it tenderly in the canoe then came back for a moment to look down upon the ashes of a dead fire. For months it had burned clear and steady and strong, but the implacable North had quenched it at last, and it could never be rekindled.

They had been six weeks going in, which tells the story of the trail they trod. Alone, Malec was two weeks reaching the crest of the height of land, but when he came to the headwaters of the Mistassini the way was easier. He drove the canoe recklessly through the rapids, and came in another week to the reservation. Straight down the lake he went, to the spot from which I had seen them come so merry and bold and gay, and drew the craft carefully up to its old place upon the shore, and when one had come to stand guard, he went to the home of the Agent. Then they went to the police, for such is the law concerning those who face the wilderness together.

"What will he do?" I asked the Agent. "Will he ever go back again?"

He did not answer for a moment, but stared moodily out across the lake. "What else can he do?" he asked then. "It is all he knows. What else is there for him to do?"

"But it would be horrible," I said, "to go back there alone."

"Yes," he said, "it will be horrible—but it is the way of the North. He will go back."

Of Flies and Such

Tomo and I were working along the shore of Lake St. John, and although it was early June when the salmon should be rising at their best, it was rather dull fishing, so I did what most salmon fishermen do under similar circumstances: I began to change flies.

Now under certain conditions such a move may be advisable, but it is a great truth that no fly is good unless it is in the water. However, I had been fishing that one long enough for it to prove its worth, so I snipped it off and took up the serious business of choosing its successor. A lot of allegedly funny stuff has been written about fishermen; but if there is anything genuinely humorous about fishing, it is that of a serious angler selecting a fly to exchange for the one he is discarding. His thoughts are mirrored in his face as he gravely extracts one from among its fellows, and holds it up to the light for a better view. That, he recalls, is the fly that took the big one on the Dumquiddy, on just such a day as this, but there's a hint of purple in the wings, and he knows that purple is anathema to salmon on an overcast day, so he goes through the books again, selecting and rejecting with all the concentration of a surgeon deciding where to make the first cut in an appendectomy. At last his face lights up as he selects a monstrosity from the bottom of the tray, and blows on it to straighten the feathers. He ties it on, works out line, being watchful of his back cast, lays the fly well out and tenses for the strike. It does not materialize, and after working the fly in for another cast he relaxes and looks down the lake to where his partner, Bill, is having the time of his life with a wildly leaping salmon. He shakes his head ruefully and digs in his fly book once more.

The foregoing is, I fear, a too accurate picture of me on that languorous morning, and I had reason to believe that so far as I was concerned, this was going to be an uneventful day.

In circumstances such as these it is well, I have found, to go ashore, cook up a bite of lunch, and lie back for an hour or so, change flies again, and wait for a rise. Tomo and I proceeded to do this, and soon the tea was simmering over a lazy fire.

It was then that I remembered the two flies that a fellow fisherman had given me that very morning at the breakfast table. The youngster had just returned from a trip to the upper falls on the Manouan. To help spread his gospel of goodwill toward men, he gave me a pair of streamers of his own design. There was nothing original about them that I could see, nor anything that looked particularly desirable, but I thanked him, dropped them into my shirt pocket, and promptly forgot them. Now I remembered them, and for want of anything better to do, I removed the old fly, bent on a dropper tag, and tied both flies to my leader. After that we doused the fire and went fishing again.

We may have paddled a quarter-mile down the shore when I had my strike. The fish took it with authority, jumped once, then splashed around on the surface in a pattern that was strictly its own. It did not jump or run but continued to flounder around in the same spot and throw water in all directions. Not until a minute had passed did it dawn on me that I had two salmon on, and that each of them was fighting its brother. When one started west, the other went east, and neither of them could gain enough slack line to enable it to jump. Except for the novelty of it, having two salmon on at the same time is only half as thrilling as it is to have only one. Still I wanted to land them, so I played them as carefully as I could, and after a few minutes had them fighting on the surface within reaching distance.

"Get the net," I said to Tomo, and Tomo said "No net."

"No net!" I cried. "Where is it?"

"On ground, I think," he said, regretfully, and I remembered then that I had removed it from the bow of the canoe when I was digging out the grub box.

Well, there we were, with two salmon which I very much wanted, splashing me with water from their position beside the canoe—and the net a quarter mile away on shore.

Now Tomo didn't have much English at his command, but he had a lot of common sense, and so I was able to put it over that I wanted him to *back* the canoe up, always keeping the bow pointed toward the fish, and to go slowly or come to a complete stop when the situation demanded it. He got the message clearly, backed carefully to our camping spot and retrieved the net, but now another problem asserted itself. The only possible way in which we could take both fish was to net the lead fish first. Otherwise a tangle of line and leaders, hooks and net would inevitably result, but he did it, scooping them up one after the other, and holding them up for me to take a swift picture before he turned them loose.

A half-hour later we repeated the little drama, only this time the net was in the canoe where it belonged. The end results, though, left something to be explained. Somewhere in the midst of the second melee the dropper fly broke off and thereafter the point fly was just a point fly with no power of its own. It is my guess that I could have picked a half-dozen combinations from my fly book that would have worked equally well, and that the worth of the pair lay in the illusion of one small fish chasing another small fish. What there was about it that made it such a hot number on the Manouan I cannot even surmise.

When a fellow has chased landlocked salmon for a quarter of a century, it is more than likely that he has formulated a few opinions concerning them. I not only have done that, but in addition I also have some preconceived notions, for my father's people had lived in the vicinity of Sebago Lake since the days when a fisherman watched with one eye strained for a rise, and the other roving the horizon for hostile Indians.

Undoubtedly such conditions lend added zest to life and enlivened many an otherwise drab day, for tradition has it that more than one of my ancestors arrived home only a jump or two in advance of a speeding tomahawk, but because of the fact that re-

sults had to be practically guaranteed, to draw a man from the safety of his own fireside, certain truisms concerning the taking of the silvery fish were not only born but also handed down to successive generations.

Thus it was that I learned to expect little sport on the lake when the wind was in the west. I strongly suspected that this superstition originated from the fact that a wind from that quarter usually made the water far too rough for any small boat, but nevertheless the idea persists in my mind even to this day, and by preference I'll take a breeze from any other quarter.

Similarly, for a long time it was believed that the salmon in Sebago fed only on smelts, and for years I pinned my faith either on the genuine article sewed on a trolling hook, or else in one of the multiple-hooked imitations. Naturally then, when I became a fly fisherman, I chose patterns that would most closely approximate the transparent little fellow and fished them to the exclusion of all others.

That fishermen as a whole are spineless vertebrates can easily be proven. Let fisherman A take a fish on a certain type of fly, and thereafter he will use nothing else, swearing his mightiest oath that it is the only fly worth a hoot in that particular body of water. Meanwhile fisherman B, using a fly as different from A's as black differs from white, also takes a fish, and loud the welkin will ring when they meet and compare notes, and instead of swapping flies and proving they are both wrong, each will stick to his theory, and loudly wail that the other is a fit candidate for the booby hatch.

Thus it was that although my fly book was crammed to its capacity, when we came once more to the lake after a week of fishing along the coast the book was practically empty. The few remaining flies were of various sizes of patterns which had proven to be best for me throughout the years, and I was convinced that they would take salmon.

The first day was disappointing. The salmon had come in from deep water, and hardly a half hour passed that I did not get a rise, or see a fish roll behind the fly, but although I succeeded in taking two fish by dinnertime, it was really poor fishing for the time and place. Methodically I began to go through the fly book, changing patterns and sizes, but I couldn't change my luck. Something was wrong, and for lack of anything better to do, I laid the blame on the wind, a soft little onshore wind that should have made every salmon in the lake ravenous.

Coming in to the lodge just as dusk was falling, we beached the canoe beside that of a young man whom I had seen going out from the lodge that morning. He was genially aglow with enthusiasm, and had a wild tale to tell of releasing a number of good fish throughout the day. I was politely skeptical, but he had his legal limit of four fine fish stored in the canoe, and they were beauties, averaging about four pounds each.

It is something of a shock to find all of one's theories knocked into a cocked hat by a mere stripling, but I recovered enough to ask him what fly he had used. He grinned apologetically and said he didn't know. He guessed they weren't any particular pattern. Just some odds and ends that he had tied himself.

I asked him to let me see them and he complied. He was right, so far as his limited description went, for they were as unorthodox as anything I had ever seen: gay, bold colors that clashed and crashed until, theoretically, they should have driven every salmon down to the bottom of the lake. He selected two entirely different ones and held them out diffidently.

"I had the best luck with these," he said. "You are welcome to try them if you care to. I'm leaving tonight."

I accepted them and thanked him as common courtesy demanded I should do, but I was not impressed with the offering. That strange things happen while fishing, his success was proof, but his monstrosities were not salmon flies. On that I would have taken my oath.

The next morning the wind blew from the south, and had increased just enough to put a beautiful ripple on the water. A faint haze hung in the distance, and a misty quality in the air presaged rain. The day was made to order for salmon fishing, and I started out with high hope. It flamed ever higher when I took a good fish before we had worked out scarcely casting distance from shore.

Fifteen minutes later I hooked another, but lost him when he did a tailspin along the surface and terminated it with a soaring leap.

"Big day today," I said to the guide, but I spoke too soon, for immediately my luck deserted me, and at ten o'clock I had not raised another fish.

Meanwhile I had been going doggedly through the fly book again, trying different patterns and size conscientiously, as a fisherman should, until I had nothing but my gift of the previous evening left to offer them. Shamefacedly I tied one on, whipped it out, and on the third cast hooked a scrappy four-pounder.

Even after it lay flopping in the canoe, I would not give credit to the fly, but attributed it to the gods of chance. However, I began to wonder when I took another fish with it a few minutes later. Anxious to prove whether the youngster had really tied some bit of magic into the garish feathers, I looped the second one on with a short tag, and laid them both close in beside a rocky point.

Instantly I saw the flash of a striking fish, and I set the hook solidly into him. He came out of water in a fine flurry that sent the spray flying, then settled back to give me as queer a battle as a salmon ever did. Time after time he would start to run, only to change his mind and terminate the rush abruptly, and when he jumped he cleared the water but feebly, like a fish already beaten.

Foot by foot I worked him in until at last the guide laid down his paddle and picked up the net. Then as the fish fought back toward him he looked quickly up.

"Two!" he said, and two there were. The flies that I had regarded so lightly had given me my first double on landlocks.

Swinging North

WHEN THE LATE Ray Schrenkeisen asked me to do the chapters on lake trout and landlocked salmon for a proposed book on the edible fishes of North America, he said, "I would like to have you distinguish between the landlocked salmon of Sebago Lake in Maine, and the *ouananiche* of Quebec. There is a difference, you know."

He was mistaken, but I didn't know it. In fact, I was not too sure that I was right in believing that *ouananiche* meant "little salmon," but Mr. Webster confirmed my guess that it was a landlocked member of the salmon clan that got lost in the shuffle during the last ice age and had never succeeded in finding its way back to the ocean. I could think of no pleasanter task than that of recording the lengths and weights of a few dozen of the renowned fighters so I accepted Ray's offer and went in search of Ernie. He is a long-time fishing companion of mine, and he fell for my proposition at once.

"Sure I'll go," he said. "It wouldn't be fair to your readers if you went up there and weighed only a few fish. We've got to do a wholesale business with them. When can we start? Tomorrow?"

With that detail taken care of, I wrote to Robertson and Son, outfitters located at Pointe-Bleue on Lake St. John, and arranged to have two guides and adequate equipment ready for a ten-day trip into the bush, beginning on June 6.

I dislike to hurry when starting a fishing trip, so we took an extra day and hired a guide to show us some of the not-so-well-known parts of the city, and especially those of the old quarter. I had been there several times previously and remember one occasion which still causes me to blush when I recall it, for at a four-way intersection in the old part of Quebec I held up the entire traffic for a whole flock of some of the longest minutes I had ever known.

Without having the faintest idea of where I wished to go, I drove into the center of the symbolic cross. Before me, a large van blocked the entire street. I chose to turn right and tried to do so but a caravan of *habitants,* their two-wheeled carts loaded to the plimsoll mark with firewood, blocked that way of escape. I craned my neck around, saw a possible way out, and swung to my left. Two motor lorries, with the insignia of the King's Army on their sides, bulked huge before me, the drivers relaxed over their steering wheels while they waited for me to make up my mind. I tried to back up but found the entire highway department parked there behind me. They had me penned in on all four sides and there was no escape. I sat there, helpless and hopeless, numbly waiting for a detachment of redcoats and a firing squad at dawn.

Ages later I stirred and glanced furtively about, and realized with a start that I was not in the United States. No fanfare of raucous horns blasted my eardrums. No leather-lunged truck driver leaned from his cab to refresh my memory of my ancestors. They looked at me curiously, as though I were a trapped animal, as indeed I was, a stupid American who was brainless and therefore blameless.

Then by some feat of magic which has not yet been made plain to me, the whole impossible scene dissolved like a fadeout in a motion picture, while carters and truck drivers beamed their appreciative thanks for the pleasant interlude I had furnished them.

The way from Quebec city to the Laurentian Mountains and the entrance of the national park is a replica of Old France. It was seed time, and the peasants were tilling the soil. I accord the French *habitant* all homage and respect. A pioneer at heart, he has learned through the centuries to avail himself of every bit of power he can extract from the creatures in his care. The summers are woefully short. I have seen the ground freeze on June 17, and frosts come again in September. Every minute must give up its full sixty seconds. Hogs rooted for grubs in what was soon to become a vegetable garden. Dogs strained in their harnesses as they drew their little carts to and from the fields. Horses, ankle deep in the soft earth, bent to their task of hauling cumbersome harrows, and frequently a bull and horse were yoked side by side and drew a plow that turned the good black earth of the fallow fields.

I wish I knew where the Frenchman finds so many women, although the knowledge would be of little value unless I also had his formula for making them work—and they certainly do work. The women were swarming like ants around the community ovens which are an integral part of every hamlet, and some were gathering in chattering bevies around the pasture bars at milking time. Unaccountably, there seemed to be at least six in each group, while children could be counted by the score. Ruddy-faced, healthy youngsters, each apparently exactly ten years old, and each smoking a villainous-looking black pipe.

The road led ever upward, and it was not long before the character of the country changed again. We were heading north, and as we crossed the mountains we were leaving spring behind. The effect was startling. Two days previously in the States we were in a land already beginning to ripple in spring's vernal green. The apple blossoms had fallen and in their place the young fruit was beginning to set. Now a half day's travel had carried us to orchards that were in full bloom, and another half day had carried us back to pink buds again. Now there were no buds, and suddenly we realized that there were no apple trees either. We had gone beyond the limit of their northern range.

The way now led up and up through the foothills, and at last bare peaks lay before us. Since the days of Jacques Cartier the mountain range had been the barrier that left the *habitant* on the southern side, but man had conquered them at last, and had driven a road up over the Laurentian Range to the fertile valley of Lake St. John. Twisting in and out through the ravines, and occasionally crawling ever and ever upward to a towering and windswept summit, a thread of road wound its way—not much of a road, I'll admit, even though the province had dwelt at length on its engineering triumphs. A footnote appended to their prospectus was illuminating. It said, in effect: "Owing to the nature of the terrain it is recommended that those who are unfamiliar with the road do not attempt its passage after dark." Sage advice indeed to be printed in letters so small.

The road was not only narrow but it had a habit of twisting in and out upon itself, or of popping up in wholly unexpected places. We climbed hogbacks that were roof-steep and from which the crests had not been shorn, and from never a sign to tell what lay just ahead. A periscope would have been invaluable, or a mast flying a white flag of surrender—anything to herald our approach, or the approach of another car headed on a collision course.

There was one breath-stopping moment when we left the lowly earth and started straight up for the top of a towering mountain peak. With infinite caution we crept out on a jutting spur, and a thousand feet of clean mountain air lay below us. In that startling void an eagle slowly wheeled on poised wings. As it swept nearer to us in its effortless orbit, I fancied that it looked at us with a speculative eye, wondering, I suppose, if we would roll free from the car if it went over the edge, and just how long it would take for our bodies to become edible if we did chance to meet with disaster.

The road has changed since that memorable day, the hogbacks have been shorn of their crests and new grades have been established, but it has only served to take away the joys of discovery. The same high peaks are there along with the same valleys, calling, as they called us then, ever onward.

Ernie's Bear

As we dropped down from the foothills of the Laurentians and came at last to a great alluvial plain, we could tell, even without the map, that we were nearing the Lake St. John country, for we knew it was a vast basin set in an amphitheater of hills. A million years ago the glaciers gouged out a great depression there, then turning southward and again toward the east cut the mighty gorge that is now the Saguenay. What turmoil of nature and what endless years went into the filling of that basin and making the inland sea that is the lake is beyond the comprehension of man, but the finished product is worth whatever it cost.

Thirty miles in length and almost equally broad, that lake is the second largest in the province. At its northern and western ends, five mighty rivers pour their waters into it. Of these five the Mistassini and the Peribonka are the largest. The Mistassini is a mile wide at its mouth. The Peribonka drains a country larger than England. So great is the volume of water flowing into it, and so mighty its exit at the Grande Décharge that the lake itself has a half-mile-per-hour current. Practically without islands, the lake is bad medicine in a blow. In that country the canoe is the one means of travel, and the Montagnais Indian is a canoeman without a peer in the whole wide world, yet I have been reliably informed that never yet has one of them tried to cross the lake. He may, and frequently does, have business upon the other side, but when that event occurs he goes the long way around. If the weather is squally (and it is more often than not in Quebec), he not only follows the shoreline but he follows it pretty closely. A few hours' time more or less doesn't mean a thing to those simple children of the forest, but they still regard life as something distinctly worthwhile. We in our higher civilization have forgotten much, I fear.

I could understand, as we came at last within sight of the lake, why the salmon that came up from the Atlantic to spawn in the cold waters of the rivers that fed the lake should decide that it was unnecessary to return again to the ocean, for the lake was immense enough to accommodate literally millions of their kind. They had remained there, and the centuries had wrought a change in them. Some vital element that the ocean carried was missing here, for the fish grew to a lesser size than did their brothers who annually came up from the salty deep, but the swift current of the lake and the tumbling waters of the rivers did something to them that compensated for their lack of weight. It molded them into trim lines that made for greater speed, and it gave them a broad and oarlike tail with which they could flash through the water and up into the air, with a succession of rushes so fast and strong that they were at once an angler's despair and joy. The leaping ouananiche (pronounce it *wa-na-neesh*,) of Lake St. John! What fisherman has not read of them and longed to pit his skill against the flashing speed of the silvery fighter? I thrilled at the nearness of the adventure, and urged Ernie to bear down a trifle harder on the gas pedal.

Life has taught me one thing. I have learned not to expect that which I fully expect to occur. In other words, to use an old aphorism, it is the unexpected that always happens.

Because firearms were barred from the park it was natural to suppose that the whole area would be literally alive with game, and pictures of game was one of the things I needed. Therefore, as soon as we entered the park I uncased the camera, guessed at the proper lens setting, rested it on the windowsill, and was ready for action.

Then I closed my eyes to give them a moment's rest and immediately tires shrieked as we came to a shuddering halt. I opened my eyes just in time to see a moose lumber out of the way as we swept around an abrupt bend, but before I could locate the shutter release he had disappeared. An open shot, and I had missed it. The folks back home would have to take my word for it. I sat up straight again and placed a forefinger on the shutter release.

Three spruce partridge burrowed in a bit of dry sand beside the road, but although they commonly show no fear of a car, they whirled away at our approach. A red fox, with a Canada jay in his mouth, whisked across before us. I think I could have stopped him with a scattergun but not with a camera. It was evident that I would never win an academy award for my photography.

So it went for ninety miles, and then the northern barrier halted us. Guards checked our papers and the contents of the car, accompanying themselves with rapid-fire French and many a shoulder shrug, then lifted the gate and let us through.

Regretfully I closed the camera case and settled back. Unless fortune favored us on our return trip there would be no pictures to show the gang back home.

We had left the Laurentians then and its seemingly interminable ranks of black spruce, and now the country became broken. The mountains had given place to hills, and the road stretched ever downward toward the Lake St. John Valley. The road improved in quality. It was wider and the grades were easier. Ernie bore down a trifle on the accelerator. We dipped down a slope, ascended a small hill, then started down an easy grade. To the left the ground sloped sharply away, while at the right it ascended at an equally sharp angle. On that side, cut squarely down where the earth had been removed, a four-foot bank marked the extreme edge of the road. We had just started the descent, when from the underbush at the left a huge bear jumped into the road and went angling across it toward the high bank. It was not the first bear I had seen in the wilds, but it was the first I had seen under such favorable circumstances. Its coat was still prime, jet black, and glossy as that of a fur seal. It rippled and gleamed as the sun struck full upon it. A trophy of which any hunter might be proud.

In watching a bear in captivity, one gathers the impression that it is cumbersome and awkward. Nothing is farther from the truth. This one moved gracefully, easily, and startlingly fast. It had about fifty feet to travel but it made the distance in not more than five jumps, and the sixth one took it up over the bank and cleanly away. I was just releasing the breath I had been holding, when Ernie cramped the wheel hard over, jammed on the brakes, set the emergency, and with a "Come on, quick!" opened the door and leaped out. I looked back to the other side of the road. In the exact path its mother had trod, a tiny cub scurried out into the road before us. The first one must have weighed three hundred pounds, for she was waist-high to a man, but this little fellow was scarcely a foot in height and would hardly have tipped the scales at five pounds. Its head, the rounded ears cocked grotesquely upward in its excitement, was huge in comparison to its absurd little body, and its legs wobbled inadequately as it scurried desperately along.

I grabbed the camera and jumped out. It was evident that this was going to be a close race, for the little fellow had a thirty-foot lead. If he topped the bank before Ernie reached him he would be safe. Ernie realized it, for he put on steam and sprinted in hot pursuit. While I fumbled blindly for the camera fastening, my eyes focused irrevocably on the drama before me.

The cub reached the bank while Ernie was yet ten feet away. Desperately it clawed its way upward, and then, just as safety lay within its reach, the grassy overhand of the bank gave away and down it came, directly between Ernie's feet. He grabbed for it, then even as his fingers were closing upon it, he hesitated and seemed to change his mind. I knew what he was thinking. Those tiny teeth were like needles, and the sheathed claws were equally sharp. There was no question concerning Ernie's ability to catch the creature. The undetermined factor was whether or not he could let go.

Clawing madly upward, the cub again reached the top of the bank and hooked a paw over it. Again the treacherous soil gave way and again the cub landed between Ernie's feet. It had been frightened before, but now terror seized it, and it whimpered like a sobbing child. Instantly a newer and more ominous sound reached my ears. Brush cracked on the hillside, and not too far away either, and a worried mother emitted a menacing growl.

I shall always believe Ernie would have grabbed it had it not been for that untimely interruption, but the threat was so ominous that it tilted the beam in the cub's favor. It scrambled up the bank again, and this time it went over the top. We had no earthly use for a bear cub, but I've always been sorry that Ernie didn't grab it. Somehow, I feel that I might have witnessed an interesting little drama. It was not more than thirty feet back to the car. I shall always believe that he could have made it. I know that I could have done so, with three hundred pounds of bear behind me.

"How many pictures did you get?" Ernie asked a half hour later, after we had recounted all the things we might have done. I looked at my camera. It was still unopened.

Black Salmon

W HEN WE ROLLED INTO Robertson's trading post at Pointe Bleue that afternoon we found a group of natives engaged in skinning a freshly killed bear, which made a total of three bears we had seen that day, a circumstance which may or may not constitute some sort of record. I would have stayed to watch the deft manner in which they peeled the pelt from the unlucky bruin except for Ernie, who goes slightly berserk whenever he is forced to stop near salmon water without having a fly rod in his hands. Grabbing an armful of equipment, and with a brief announcement of "I'm going fishing," he signaled to an Indian who seemed to be waiting for a bit of lucrative labor, and within ten minutes of the time when we arrived, he had a salmon on and was making the welkin ring with his happy yell.

I went back to Robertson's trading post, where Tommy, the "Son" part of Robertson and Son, greeted me with typical French courtesy, and laid out a tentative schedule. The salmon, he said, had just commenced to come in from the deeper waters offshore and were beginning to riot in the shallows where the bait fish were accumulating. It might interest us, he thought, to put in a day or two right there at the lodge while we fished through the daylight hours, and then spend some time in the evening watching the trappers come in with their furs. It proved to be the highlight of the next two days, for the trapping season had been one of the best in years for quantity of pelts, while the high quality was plainly visible, even to my untrained eye.

There was an abundance of beaver pelts, a fact that was doubly pleasing, for I could remember only a few decades earlier that conservationists had declared that the beaver was perilously near extinction. Now they were plentiful enough to justify the trappers' truism that when beaver were plentiful other furs would also be found in greater quantities.

I was amazed at the variety of furs. Some, such as the muskrat and mink, I could identify, but the fishers and martens were new to me, as were the black muskrats from Ungava. There were enough of the ubiquitous white weasels and other exotic furs to clothe all royalty—and with a few packloads to spare.

It was here that I learned to forever banish from my mind the belief that the trader had the trapper irrevocably in his power. The grim picture, as the sob sisters painted it, was that of a trapper dumping his pack of pelts on the trading room floor at the Hudson's Bay Post, and then going out to imbibe enough alcohol to float his laden canoe before he returned to learn what price his winter's work. Nothing is further from the truth. It may be that in the old days there was occasionally a Shylock who demanded his pound of flesh, but those days are now gone forever. The spruce forests that once were sawed into lumber are now ground into pulp which is made into paper that feeds the presses of the world. Unfortunately—from the buyer's standpoint—the papers eventually find themselves circulating through the reservation, and the Indian has learned to read. By that manner he has learned to keep a tab on current prices, and woe betide the buyer who tries a bit of chicanery. In order to do business he must have furs to sell, and if he does not go along with the trapper on price he may find that someone else has skimmed the cream off the lot, leaving him to hold the almost empty bag.

Still another factor which may cause him some sleepless nights is the ever-present fear that he has bought on a falling market, which leaves him dangling between the upper and nether mill-stones, and if he cannot raise cash to cover his liabilities bank-ruptcy is his only way out. One buyer told me mournfully that one season he had been taken to the tune of $50,000, but his face lightened considerably when he told me that his greatest profit for a single deal came from the one for which he paid $72,000 to a family consisting of the trapper, his squaw, and four grown sons. By seemingly common consent the squaw took charge of the money, carrying it about in a voluminous pocket in her dress. When one of the family requested a bit of petty cash he was given the outside bill of the roll, whether it was a five or a fifty, and when the buyer advised putting the money in the bank at Roberval, she refused on the grounds that "If the man on the bank die I no get my money": a not too farfetched assumption at that.

The allegation that a victimized trapper might seek solace in drink is nonsense. He is, in a sense, a government ward, and to sell liquor to him would be be a felony. Boiled down to its essentials is the fact that the Montagnais trapper has about the best form of social security that can be found in any civilized nation today. If weeping is in order, let the tears be shed for the poor trapper who has no paternal government to back him in his ventures, but leaves him to survive or perish by his own efforts. If he sometimes downgrades a pelt or two—and gets away with it—all power to him, I say.

For two days Ernie and I had the sort of fishing that is commonly found only in dreams, playing fifty-three salmon in all. We handled them carefully at times in order to determine just how light the tackle could be and still be effective. At other times we played it rough and learned that it was folly to keep a tight line on a jumping fish—especially on the occasional five-pounder—for he would invariably fall on the taut leader and break it.

Remembering Schrenkeisen, we weighed and measured each fish and returned it unharmed to the water. The average weight of the fifty-three was 2¾ pounds. The largest of the lot pulled the scale down to the six-pound mark. Let it be known that a six-pound ouananiche is a good ouananiche in any man's favorite puddle.

Just how long we would have continued our orgy is problematical, for sometime in our second day a typical St. Lawrence Valley northeaster came storming in to effectively stop all fishing in the big lake, for much of the water on the eastern shore is shallow and turns a rich coffee color after a few hours of heavy wind.

Although highly improbable, it is still possible for a bone-weary fly-fisherman to lay down his implements of war for an hour or two if compelled to do so for any reason, but he paces the floor like a caged animal whenever a storm forces him ashore. So it was with us when the northeaster blew in. The prospect of sitting around for two or three fishless days was appalling, for there was no way by which we could tell when the wind would stop. Something drastic was called for. We hunted up the guides.

"Where," I asked Joe, a lanky guide under whose care I had been for the preceding days, "is there a pond or river small enough so the wind will not bother us? A river with salmon in it. Plenty salmon. Do you know such a place?"

Joe conferred with Tommy but all I could glean was that Lake James wouldn't be rough because it was long and narrow. There were, they alleged, plenty salmon but they were black. *Noir!* Black like the night. Furthermore, they "no take fly," but must be dredged from the bottom with worms or bait fish, after the manner of taking namaycush, or lake trout.

Well, part of our assignment was to get additional data on lake trout, and Lake James might be a good place from which to gather it. But the black salmon story was a difficult pill to swallow. I wondered if they would be telling us next about white lampblack, buckets of steam, and left-hand monkey wrenches, but there was no telltale lurking grin to give them away. I looked at Ernie, and he nodded a go-ahead signal.

"All right," I told Joe. "Pack plenty tents, plenty blankets, plenty food for three or four days. We are going to have a look at your black salmon."

Now the word "black" when used in connection with salmon

connotes inferiority, and is commonly used when referring to sea salmon which have remained in the river after spawning. There, with no salt water to brighten and invigorate them, they become dark and unattractive in appearance, a ghastly example of what a wrong environment may do to any creature wearing fur, fins, or feathers.

The belief which is now universally accepted is that mammoth Lake St. John serves as an ocean for the Lake James fish; that they winter in the shallows, and spend their summers in the deepest part of the abnormally deep Lake James.

The belief seems logical enough, but whatever the cause may be, the fish were there in soul-satisfying size and numbers. And they were black. There could be no mistaking that fact. And they were as full of fight as tiger sharks. Also, despite what the guides had told us, these salmon took several kinds of streamer flies, particularly those that most closely resembled the native smelts. We found the most exciting way to take them was to cruise around waiting for a rise and then cast to the ring. When we got the fly there quickly enough, it almost always produced a rise, and the resultant battle was unique in my experience.

Bottom was sixty feet down, and that was where the fish wanted to be. When hooked, they usually made a short run that terminated in a leap, and then they bored straight down with a power that no light fly rod could stop. Although the fight was never spectacular, the salmon still gave the fisherman his money's worth. The minute-per-pound rule did not not apply here, for the fish were all in the four- to five-pound class.

Remembering Schrenkeisen, we skinned a dozen fish, salted the skins heavily, and packed them to take home as evidence if we were accused of perjury.

Only one thing prevented our day from being a perfect one.

Tommy had made a slight error in assigning guides to several other parties. Joe was to be our head man, and we were to pick up the second one—a newly returned trapper—on the way in to the lake, but when we arrived there we found that he had failed to get the message clearly over the wire telephone and was in the bush, setting bear traps. Bears, we found, were playing an unexpected part in our lives.

All was not lost, however. Partway up the lake, Joe disclosed, we would find an Indian family consisting of a father, a son, a plump squaw, and innumerable small fry of various sizes. Father and son were newly returned from the trapline, and the boy, John, would gladly go to man a canoe and help on the portages. It was far from the setup we had expected, but there was little that we could do about it now. "All right," we said, "tell the boy to come along. We'll look after him."

Even yet I blush with shame when I think of that moment.

Look out for him, indeed! John was nineteen years old and was built like a young sandow. His face was pleasing, as were those of the brothers and sisters that lined up at the water's edge; a little curious, but poised for instant flight, like the young wood creatures that they were.

One could not help liking them all at sight, but it was John that I wanted for my very own. I could see that he welcomed the opportunity to go with us, for he went quickly up the bank and as quickly returned. A light jersey for extra clothing, a canoe, and a pair of paddles were all the preparation he made for an as yet undetermined numbers of days, but in the brief minutes while we rearranged the load in the two canoes, I appraised the youngster and made my decision. Whether by hook or by crook I was going to have this fellow for my very own. It proved to be a happy choice.

Choosing a first-class canoeman from among the throng of *habitants* is akin to picking a winning ticket on the Irish Sweepstakes. I do not mean to imply that the native Frenchman is not a good canoeist. Far from it. He is among the world's best, but the niceties of using a light fly rod are beyond his comprehension.

It is probable that more fish are lost at the net than at any other stage of the battle simply because the canoeman failed to keep his angler headed toward his fish. There is nothing more disconcerting to a fisherman than to find himself holding the rod over his shoulder in the manner of a baseball bat, while the guide has laid his paddle across the thwarts and is methodically loading his pipe. It would never occur to him in a hundred years to turn the canoe so that the angler may face the fish. As a matter of fact, he has but little interest in fly-rod fishing as a means of staving off starvation, when the feat could be accomplished in one-tenth the time and effort by using a handline. By the same standard half a canoeload of fish taken overnight in a gill net would be the acme of sport for him. For the long-drawn-out battle in which the temper of a light rod and the stretch of a delicate leader must not be forgotten for a moment, he has absolutely no use. He seems to regard it as an expression of a feebler intellect, as perhaps it is, and he would be happy if he could convert you to his belief.

We found the Indians to be delightfully different.

Mountain Trout

THERE WERE PLENTY of salmon in Lake James. Big hungry fellows that moved endlessly about in search of food and filled the vast morning and evening stillness with their splashings. Sometimes, after night had fallen and the wind stilled, we would lie in the tent and listen to the resounding thump as a big fellow leaped clear of the water in his rush for a luckless minnow. Sounds like that are sweet music to the ear of a fisherman, and we should have been entirely happy. Driven as we were from the big lake by the northeaster that still moaned and sighed across the crests of the hills that towered all around us, we had hit this glory hole at a time when the salmon were taking at their best. To be discontented at such a time was little short of treason, but, nevertheless, even while I rubbed the cramps from a wrist that twenty minutes of fast and furious fighting had rendered agonizingly painful, I was aware of a disquieting feeling of unrest. It persisted through all the first day and the second, and it was well into the middle of the third before I discovered the cause.

Joe had told us about the trout pond that lay over there beyond the black hills, and it was this that was bothering me. A natural trout hole that hadn't been fished for four years. Four years! A brook trout can put on a lot of poundage in that length of time. Thinking about it, I remembered the pair of nine-pounders in the Commissioner's office at Quebec. Undoubtedly there were some big fish left in the pond when it was last fished, and now, after four years, they should have doubled in weight. A salmon, threshing open-mouthed through a school of smelts, broke water and dashed spray against the side of the canoe, but I let it go unmolested upon its way. There was something infinitely more important than salmon.

"Have you ever been in to that trout pond?" I asked John.

He ceased paddling for a moment and his even, white teeth showed in a quick and pleasing smile.

"Okay," he said.

"How far is it there?"

"Okay," he answered.

I knew he didn't understand a word that I was saying, but at a time like that, when I was about to decide to leave a glorious certainty for something as uncertain as only trout fishing can be, I needed a bit of moral support.

"What do you think our chance would be for taking some big trout if we hiked in there?" I asked him.

"Okay," he promptly answered. I had liked him from the first, but now my liking was growing into a warm and personal regard. This young fellow knew his stuff. His instantaneous corroboration of my suggestion was proof of that.

"We're going in there tomorrow," I said.

"Okay," he answered, and it was settled.

I announced my decision to Joe that night, but he was not overly enthusiastic. "Hard portage," he said. "Trail grown up and tree fall over him. Very bad."

"We'll send John in to clear it," I said. Three miles of rough trail was not going to stop me, now that I had made up my mind. Four years was far too long for any trout pond to go unfished, even if three times three miles of unbroken forest guarded it.

Joe was the perfect head guide. He had voiced his objection but now my wish was law. He would execute it not only efficiently but cheerfully. He turned to the Indian and relayed the command.

John was off at sunrise the next morning, a camp ax and a lunch that he packed in my trout basket his sole equipment. From where we sat, as we ate breakfast, I could watch him as he paddled down the lake. There was no hesitation in his paddle stroke, but he drove steadily onward until the morning mists had swallowed him. "He never been on that place," Joe had told me, "but he find it." I think that it was then that I gained a new perception of the superb woodsmanship that is the northern Indian's inheritance. I spread our map of that country across my knees, and in all that vast emptiness that was the country in which we were, the nameless little pond did not occupy a place large enough to be designated by the mark of a pencil point, yet John's confident departure told me that he would surely find his way back again. It was a gift peculiar to his race, and all that tremendous expanse that stretched northward to the shores of Hudson's Bay was to them exactly what my backyard was to me. It was home.

That day we doubled up in the one remaining canoe. Again the salmon were ravenous. They took almost everything we offered them and they fought as only landlocks can fight, but I think I had never known a longer day. The sun's rays were beginning to tell at last and there was a springlike warmth in the the air. It was getting to be trout weather, and my mind's eye could picture nothing but that little pond.

It was deep dusk when John returned. I caught the flash of his paddle far down the lake and I was again impressed by the fellow's marvelous physique, for even at that distance I could see the dancing craft surge ahead as he drove it tirelessly toward us. He came in, spoke briefly to Joe, grinned at us, then turned to the fire.

"He cleared the portage," Joe informed us. "You go tomorrow, no?"

"We go tomorrow, yes," I corrected him. "Early."

For four days the wind had been blowing steadily from the northeast. Now it swung abruptly in the northwest and brought a frigid chill with it. There were a pair of four-point Hudson's Bay blankets on our bed, but they were none too many. In the morning the ground was white with frost and there was a skim of ice in the water pail—on the seventeenth of June, too. I thought of those pioneers who were still clearing land but a few miles behind us and wondered what crops they could ripen before mid-September when the ground would freeze again. Well, that was their worry. Mine concerned something more important. This wasn't trout weather, not with the Arctic wind shrieking around us. Still, trout could grow reasonably hungry in four years. I decided to go through with it, even though Ernie was not too enthusiastic concerning the plan. He was a salmon fisherman and he had been finding it here in soul-satisfying quantity. His objections were only half-hearted ones that were based on wisdom, but wisdom has seldom entered into my fishing plans. We departed at once.

Two miles down the lake we pulled ashore. High hills ran down to the water's edge, so steeply slanted that to get out and draw the canoe ashore was something of a problem. We made it, however, and lashing the paddles to the thwarts for shoulder rests, John swung the canoe aloft and struck out. In that dense forest of almost impenetrable spruce he was instantly out of sight.

Joe's light pack contained a loaf of bread, a slab of bacon, and a frying pan. Ernie carried our case of fly rods. My burden consisted of my camera and a landing net, but I speedily found that they were too much. I had envisioned a well-marked trail from which all hindering obstacles had been removed, but again I had erred. Hundreds of fallen spruces barred our way. If one was waist-high, John had chopped it in two and permitted the ends to drop down into the trail. If one had lodged at a lesser height, it was permitted to lie there unmolested. John's six-foot height was achieved in part by a pair of extremely long legs, but how any man could step over such obstacles while burdened with seventy pounds of canoe, climbing steadily up a steep mountain side, and manage to keep so far ahead that he was beyond both sight and hearing was something to wonder at.

We struggled and panted on, over a trail that was no trail,

across watercourses that were reminiscent of a giant's stairway, so high and far apart were the steppingstones. We scrambled along the sides of ravines so steep that one false step would have sent us plunging down to the bottom, and then we crossed them on single, springy spruce logs to other equally hazardous ways on the other side. The trail, I learned, was cleared not upon the ground but six feet above it. John's problem was not where to plant his feet but how to get the overturned canoe through the tangle. To balance himself upon a single log above a ten-foot drop was nothing, but to have that balance disturbed by a limb brushing along the side of the canoe while he was doing it was something that had to be considered. I began to pick out the trail by watching for the openings high above the ground, from which the limbs had been lopped off by John's ax on the previous day.

Even with that evidence it was hard to believe that he was really before us, for it seemed physically impossible for any man so burdened to make such speed, but here and there in a bit of soft earth I saw the imprint of a moccasined foot, pressed to an extra depth by the added weight of the canoe, and I knew that he was still ahead of us, even though no sound came back to us.

Dimly within me, resentment began to take form. I passed Joe and quickened my pace. The Indian was only human, as was I. I proposed to catch up with him and witness the marvelous foot-work that was carrying him so swiftly and so surely over these impossible places.

The Little Great Divide

THE TRAIL TO the nameless trout pond was, as I have intimated, breathtakingly uphill. My knowledge of the country was exceedingly limited, but I was soon to learn that this rocky, rugged elevation was not a mountain as I had supposed, but rather the long, narrow height of land that separates eastern and western Quebec.

For the moment, though, I was more interested in anthropology than geology. Somewhere ahead of me in the dark and gloomy forest was a superman, a throwback to the muscular, primitive creature that roamed these hills when the world was young. Resting upon his shoulders was a seventy-pound canoe, but that was not his only handicap. The craft was almost four feet wide and eighteen feet long. To carry it around the endless corners and up all the ravines and watercourses through which the path led was something worthy of mention, but to carry it at a pace that completely outdistanced my camera-laden self was something that approached the miraculous. It was a challenge that I could not ignore. The Indian had the advantage of me in years, but I was neither antiquated nor decrepit. I could follow a bird dog from dawn to dusk for days on end, and my legs would still function at the end of the period. In addition, I had now learned to read the faint signs of the trail. The overhanging branches lopped from the spruces, the little squares of birch bark that John had dropped on the previous day to mark the abrupt bends, the natural openings caused by the bare rocks—these were all the guideposts one needed. I opened my shirt at the throat, tightened my belt another notch, scurried around Ernie, and struck out at my best pace.

I had fancied we were nearing the crest of the rise, but now, perhaps because of my haste, the way seemed to grow steeper and infinitely rougher. The melting snow of countless centuries, and the torrential rains that swept up the St. Lawrence Valley in the spring, had successfully prevented the accumulation of any surface soil, and the rocks stood out bold and bare to form a barrier more formidable to my feet than were the fallen trees over which I had been scrambling, but nevertheless I forced myself to a still faster pace. If I did not overtake John's fleeing form among these almost insurmountable obstacles, I was convinced I would not see him until I reached the lake.

Minutes passed, and then I knew that the forest was thinning out. Until that moment the interlaced branches of the spruces

214

had effectually shut out the bitter northwest wind, but now I could feel it swooping down around me, piercing my clothing and chilling my perspiring flesh. Suddenly the trees were gone and a last short ascent of bare rock lay before me. I scrambled up over it and stopped to look down upon the world. North and south the ridge ran, stretching as far in either direction as the eye could see, while to the east and west it dropped away to lesser ridges and endless valleys. I looked westward. The descent was more gradual there and strangely bare of vegetation. A quarter-mile below, where the spruces should have again claimed possession, tall whitened poles stood starkly out from among a sea of newly leaved ferns and blueberry bushes. It was evident that a shattered lightning bolt had started a conflagration not many years previously, and while I stood there looking at it, thinking how those whitened spars resembled the masts of the returned fishing fleet in old Gloucester, I caught a momentary flash of sunlight on what I knew to be the varnished surface of the canoe. It was more than a quarter mile away and it vanished with disconcerting suddenness. John had rounded the turn and was going into the home stretch. A falcon hawk or a well-trained greyhound might possibily have caught him, although I would have been inclined to take the short end of any bet to that effect, but of one thing I was absolutely sure. No creature that moved on two legs could do it in the length of time left at his disposal. I knew when I was beaten. Picking out a rock that looked to be at least as soft as any of its fellows, I sank down on it and awaited the arrival of the more sensible members of our little party.

They came up presently, Ernie slightly red of face, and mopping himself industriously and continuously with a limp handkerchief, and Joe phlegmatically bringing up the rear, his wrinkled and leathery skin still bone-dry, but with a look of veiled amusement in his sleepy eyes.

"No catch him, eh?" he asked.

"N-no." Even so short a sentence was still too long for a single breath.

"He big fellow," Joe said. "Much strong."

I agreed with him. I thought then, and still think that with a year's training in the art of boxing, John could have made any of the heavyweight contenders for the title look like rankest of rank amateurs. Of one thing I am absolutely certain. None of them could have caught him had he chosen to keep out of their reach.

"You come," Joe said, "I show you fonny t'ing."

He struck off northward along the crest of the ridge and we followed him. A few hundred yards ahead we came to a slight moss-grown depression in which a shallow little pond danced and rippled before the whipping wind. Its total area was scarcely more than a half acre, and I was wondering at the vagaries of a nature capable of placing a spring in such an impossible place, when I became aware that Joe was again speaking.

"Two way she go," he said, stretching his arm in a sweeping gesture toward the east and west. "Fonny t'ing, no?"

I opened my map, and sure enough he was right. From the point where we stood, a tiny thread ran eastward to connect with James River, and merge with it to wind its way at length into the Mistassini, then into the Saguenay and down into the Gulf of St. Lawrence. To the south a similar thread ran, trickling down the slope to join other rivulets that became brooks, which eventually found their way into the St. Lawrence, hundred of miles above the lower outlet.

I made a note of it there, that someday I might ponder upon

216

the mysterious providence that could separate two companionable little raindrops, and then reunite them months later, somewhere out in the mighty Atlantic, but now a more pressing urge
was upon me. I wanted to get down to the little pond where no
fly-fisherman had been in four long years. I wanted to assemble
my rod, tie on a strong leader and the most gaudy fly in the
book, then go out and whip the waters to a creamy froth, and see
what happened. After that, when at last the time came to depart and
John had again lifted the canoe to his shoulders, I wanted to fall in
about twenty feet behind him and maintain that distance until we
reached the lake or until I dropped from utter exhaustion.

The years have taught me one thing. If a fellow concentrates
hard enough, or wishes hard enough, some of his wishes will be
granted.

The Foot Race

Now THAT WE HAD SCALED the mountain height, the trail generously obeyed a law of nature and wound its way downhill. It was a welcome relief after the long climb, and we hurried eagerly along. At last we neared a clearing in the bottom of the first valley, and through it we caught the glint of sunlight on the water that had cost all these aching muscles.

It was an insignificant little pond, not much more than a stone's throw across and only two or three times as long, but I knew it was the place we were seeking, for the canoe reposed right-side up on the shore, and John was perched jauntily upon its stern smoking his reward for the effort, a hand-rolled cigarette.

218

One may, if he is of a particularly generous nature and taxes his mind long enough, find a few things to say in favor of the Canadian version of the fragrant weed. Its construction lends itself readily to a workman's conception of what a plug of tobacco should really be, and it permits itself to be molded into something that strongly resembles an elongated and slightly decomposed Vienna loaf. It weighs less for its bulk than anything else in the world except a fully inflated dirigible, and is the only life preserver a native canoeman ever carries. I have been reliably informed that a single plug of it has supported the combined weight of two men for hours in the water, and that on more than one occasion when a cataract has suddenly deprived a lone voyageur of his conveyance, he has pulled one of those remarkable contributions to science from his pocket, climbed astride it, and nonchalantly paddled himself ashore.

There are several so-called tobacco cures on the market, but I'll wager my all that none of them ever began to compare with this simple sun-dried remedy. My personal opinion is that it is the one and only infallible panacea for any ailment. The first pipeful raises a great question in one's mind, and the second one definitely answers it. It strikes at the very root of the disease, and instead of creating a desire for something with nicotine in it, it makes the very thought of the drug particularly abhorrent. I have been told that it takes seventeen years of constant application to the task to acquire a real yearning for the stuff, and that if the exigencies of the trail suddenly deprives an addict of his supply for a period of five days, he is forced to begin at scratch and work for an additional seventeen years. To me, it seems hardly worthwhile.

John, however, had both the physique and inborn determination so necessary to achieve success. He was sitting as I have said, upon the stern of the canoe, gulping great quantities of the acrid smoke into his lungs. As we assembled our rods and feverishly threaded our lines through the guides, he grinned charmingly at us.

Fishing is an obsession, and the sight of even a modest and unpretentious body of water will stir a devotee's emotions to an almost uncontrollable pitch, but this pond was as seductive and alluring as Cleopatra. The shore where we stood was comparatively flat, but much of that which remained was abrupt and gave an impression of the cool depths so necessary for a trout paradise on a hot midsummer's day. Here and there around the pond's irregular permimeter great slabs of granite stood boldly above the surface, or slanted obliquely down to afford a sun parlor that would be welcomed by all the finny tribe on a day like this. The weariness of the trail departed like magic from our muscles, and we were primitive creatures scenting the presence of food and anxious for the kill.

The question as to which of us should have first use of the canoe was not easy to answer, but we solved the problem by the age-old method of drawing for short straws. Ernie won, as I knew he would, for he has mastered the art of snapping the tough fiber between his fingers and doing it so unobtrusively and with such a saintly look on his face that one is half glad he broke his own selection an inch longer than he intended. I watched them depart, with Joe perched precariously high on the stern. Then I gathered up my rod and fly book and worked my way down the shore to where two giant rocks formed the formation I sought. The first, a flat table top, projected several feet above the water, while the second upreared itself behind it to form an effectual windbreak and a welcome reflector of the sun's rays. John, loyally attached to me again after our separation on the trail, lay comfortably curled at the base of the rock.

I waited while Ernie and Joe made their way down to the lower end of the pond, where the higher walls broke the force of the wind and made casting less difficult. They had the advantage over me—but just show me a trout fisherman who can stand for more than a minute or two beside a trout pool and manage to keep his line and leader dry. The boulder at my back prevented casting in the conventional manner, but the roll cast was invented for use in just such places. I stood well out on the edge of the rock and worked out a respectable length of line.

All the hope that buoys up the soul of a fisherman stirred within me as I made that first cast. Surely after four unmolested years, the trout would have gained both formidable size and appetite. I grasped the rod firmly as I started a slow retrieve, expecting some mighty old warrior would wrest it from my grasp.

There is no thrill greater than that of taking the first sizable fish from new waters, and there is no disappointment keener than that of learning that one has again erred in his judgment concerning the correct time and place. The latter was my lot. For two hours Ernie and I whipped the waters with unremitting zest, then we changed places and kept at it for another hour, but to no avail. Then we stored our rods in their cases and prepared to depart, beaten as we had been beaten so many times before. But for me the day was not yet done. I waited, and when John tossed the canoe to his shoulders, I looked at my watch and swung in close behind him. This time I meant business. It had been foolish of me to insist on coming here in such weather, but if I could match the pace set by this superman and be right there behind him when he set the canoe down in the big lake, my self-respect would be restored, and the day would not be so utterly spoiled.

What followed thereafter has never seemed real to me, but more like a nightmare in which I alternately ran and fell, only to rise up and run and fall again. It was these falls that beat me, for even though I scrambled to my feet as fast as possible after each crash, I invariably lost a few precious seconds. Almost imperceptibly the distance between us widened. At first it was only a matter of inches: then the inches grew into feet and the feet into yards, and no power within me could prevent it. When we reached the crest of the rise he was a gunshot ahead, but on the downward stretch I held my own, for when I caught the first glimmer of water through the trees I saw him step into the opening and ease the canoe gently down. I stopped and looked at my watch. Exactly fifty minutes had elapsed.

He had a cigarette rolled and lighted when I reached him. He looked fresh and fit, as though the distance had been rods rather than miles. He breathed evenly and unhurriedly. His skin showed no trace of moisture.

"You're some man, John," I panted admiringly. He grinned at me, a friendly and companionable grin.

"Okay," he said.

Lake Trout Eldorado

IF ANYONE HAD TOLD ME a few days earlier that the time would ever come when I tired of catching salmon I would have advised him to seek a phrenologist, but for several days we had caught and weighed and released more of the Lake James black salmon than we could have found in the States in an entire season. There was absolutely no fishing pressure on the lake, for the term "black" in relation to salmon is a dirty one that connotes to Atlantic salmon anglers a fish that has remained in the river after spawning and is a disreputable-looking character when the ice goes out in the spring.

To the Lake James salmon, though, the lake represents the ocean, and from its depths we took a score of fat fish whose beauty was beauty of form rather than color. We smoked a half dozen over our campfire to preserve them until we could ice them for the trip home, weighed and recorded a dozen for Schrenkeisen's book, and then began to look around for other worlds to conquer. In the back of my mind the words "Lake Alex" kept trying to forge to the front, for I had a faint remembrance that some remarkable lake trout had been hauled from its crystal-clear waters, and lake trout were on our agenda, but we wondered if there was not a smaller and nearer lake in the immediate area where we could take a few good fish for comparison. I consulted Joe about it and struck oil the first thing. Joe consulted John. John consulted his oracle, and after a minimum of pointing and arm waving they both consulted me. Only one short mile away, Joe reported, was a pond so full of lake trout that it was bursting over its banks. Unless the water level could be lowered by dragging out a few thousand fish, disaster was sure to result. We owed a debt to Canada and it must be paid.

It seemed too good to be true, so we grabbed our rods, a canoe, and struck off for the lake trout Eldorado.

The way, Joe had promised, was gratifyingly level, and there was a faintly defined moose path to aid us, and in a surprisingly short time we were there. A moose, whether cow or bull I could not tell, grazed knee-deep on the lily bulbs around it, and Joe bewailed the fact that he didn't have a rifle.

"Look, Joe," I said, "there's a fire warden somewhere around, and he would hear the shot. What would he say when he found you skinning a freshly killed moose?"

Joe shrugged unconcernedly. "He say nothing, he answered. "He know I use the meat. He no say anything."

"What would he say if I shot it?" I asked.

Joe's eyes crinkled at the corners. "He say something then," he said.

I was assembling my rod when a piteous moan from Ernie stopped me.

"Where," he demanded, "is my tackle box? Where are all the big hooks and weighted lines? Where is all the lake trout gear? Where is almost everything?"

"An apt question," I said. "They are up at the head of the lake where we left the car, and I'm not going to draw lots again to see who goes after them. We'll make do with what we have."

"All right," Ernie said, "but I know how it is going to work out. If there are any fish here, they are going to be in the deep water, so Joe says, and with these fly-casting lines we can't get down there. We might as well give it up, unless—" He moved away mumbling to himself.

"Unless what?" I asked.

"Look," said Ernie, "why can't we cut the backing off your line and tie it to mine? That will give us an extra forty yards."

"There are two reasons why you can't cut my line," I told him. "The first reason is that it's my line. The second is that the reel will not hold it."

"It will hold most of it," he persisted.

"What good will that do us? Unless it holds all of it, it might as well not hold any. What will you do with fifteen or twenty yards of line and fish dangling from the end of a fly rod, I'd like to ask? Go ashore and drag it in?"

"Didn't you ever hear of stripping in line?" There was a hint of sarcasm in his tone.

"Sure, I've heard of it," I said. "And didn't you ever hear that it was one of the nicest ways in the world to break a fifty-dollar rod? Or were you planning to use my rod, as well as my line?"

"Listen," he said. "We've got to get down after those big boys some way, and we can't very well dive that deep. What do you say?"

There is, I think, some merit in looking on the negative side of a forlorn hope, for in summing up the possibilities of failure one stands an infinitely better chance to succeed. Now that we had looked at the dark side of the matter, I answered as I had intended to do from the first. "Of course we'll use it," I agreed. "What's a fly line or two between friends?"

Uncoiling the lines, we made the splice, but when we rewound it once more at least thirty feet of line refused to go back on the spool. "It's all right," Ernie said. "I'll manage some way." He seized the can of minnows, stepped in, and they were off.

Left to amuse ourselves as best we could, I fell to talking again to John, for I felt that his repertoire of one English word should have at least one daily workout.

"Do you know how to call moose?" I asked him.

"Okay," he said.

He had seated himself on a boulder and with his pocketknife was busying himself making a boy's whistle from a piece of sappy moosewood. He slipped the bark off cleanly, gouged out a businesslike sound chamber, and slid the cover back into place.

"Well, call one," I commanded.

"Okay," he replied, and putting the whistle to his lips he blew a plaintive note like that of a homesick sandpiper.

"Look here," I said. "You can't call a moose with that thing. What you need is a birchbark horn and a knowledge of moose

dialect. Um-m-ph——um-m-ph! Wa-a-ah! You call. Moose come. No?"

His face lit up at once and he smiled his seraph's smile. "Okay," he answered and disappeared into the forest. He was back presently with a roll of bark which he twisted into a mega- phone. Placing it to his lips, he bent over until the tip of the horn was scarcely a foot from the ground. Filling his chest then, he cut loose. The moosewood leaves trembled and danced, and a mighty and dissonant volume of sound went tearing across the lake. "AR-r-ah! Arr-ruh! Ah-we-a-aw!" Such a noise as one might expect to hear from a Metropolitan basso profundo in the throes of acute indigestion, but never from the gentle-voiced, soft-spoken John. The earth trembled from the force of it, and when it was over I spoke hastily.

"Enough of that is altogether too much," I told him. "Go back to your whistle, my boy."

"Okay," he said, and would have responded with an encore, but I restrained him forcibly and led him back to his neglected instrument. He picked it up and tooted it happily, while I turned to look at the distant canoe. Ernie had a fish on! I could tell from the way Joe sat in the stern, with has paddle poised for instant ac- tion, and from the sun's glint upon a fly rod that was now a qui- vering crescent. I watched with interest, and when I saw Joe dig his paddle deep and send the canoe dancing away I knew that a big fish was making a determined run.

Through it all, John had continued his piping, and now sud- denly all the swallows in the Dominion were there in front of us. They formed a blue cloud that banked and swooped and eddied and swirled, chirruping advice and sympathy to the luckless one of their kind that they were apparently convinced was being held

228

prisoner by the giant redskin. I began to have a new respect for the soft-voiced chap. If he could call birds to him in such numbers, what could he do in good moose country in late September when the hot blood coursed madly through the veins of the warring old bulls? Then and there I made a vow that someday I would come back and find out.

When I looked out on the lake again I saw that the canoe was drawing in toward shore. The battle had been a short one after all. The conquering hero was coming in to display his spoils. Evidently I was in for a bit of well-deserved razzing. Who was I to say that big lake trout could not be taken by stripping line in by hand?

The canoe touched the shore and Ernie climbed out. There was a wild light in his eye but his hands were empty.

"Aren't there any big hooks in your kit?" he asked.

"Big hooks? You had a card of 2's. What bigger do you want?"

"I want cod hooks," he said. "Something that will hold real fish."

"Number 2's will hold any fish in Canada," I told him, and then launched my barbed shaft. "That is, it will hold him if he is played properly."

He winced a trifle, but smiled good-naturedly. "Maybe you think you could play one properly with this outfit."

"The outfit wasn't my idea," I reminded him. "What's wrong with it?"

"Not much," he said. "It's all right, only the rod isn't stiff enough to set a hook properly; it's hard work to get the greased line down to the bottom, and the reel is too small. Otherwise it's all right."

"A good workman can do a good job with poor tools," I quoted. With that, I picked up my tackle box, stepped into the canoe, motioned to Joe to get out, and to John to take his place. "It's the man behind the gun that really counts," I said. "Shove off, John."

Ernie was right concerning the difficulty in getting the line down. It needed a heavy lead, but these we did not have. However, I squeezed a few more split shot on the stout leader, to supplement those he had already fixed to it, replaced the cleanly broken hook with another of similar size, threaded a minnow upon it, and began to pay out line.

Slowly John worked the canoe out into deep water while I let the line run free. The oiled silk disappeared astern and then yard after yard of backing ran out until a well-remembered knot appeared. That would be the hasty splice we had made. It meant that seventy yards were dragging behind us and that about forty more remained on the spool. With any sort of luck it should be enough. I thumbed the revolving spool to stop its turning and estimated the speed at which we were traveling. "A little slower, John," I said.

"Okay," he answered and quickened the pace.

"No! No! I remonstrated. "Slower!"

"Okay," he repeated, and the canoe leaped ahead.

Then it happened.

Namaycush

ONE OF THE MANY complexities that enter every man's daily life is his imagination, and nowhere does it run so unbridled as in the field of sports. The upland bird hunter is galvanized into instant action when a chicadee flutters on a branch. The wildfowler crouches in his blind and freezes into immobility when a tiny speck moves on the horizon, while every fluttering branch and weathered stump is a potential deer to the big-game hunter.

A fisherman is similarly handicapped. Let his dragging line touch a floating bit of driftwood ever so lightly and he is instantly tensely alert. If the trailing bait becomes momentarily entangled with a gossamer bit of pond weed, his nerve reflexes instantly respond and he jerks sharply on the rod. Let a sinker bump bottom and his heart will leap to his throat as his imagination pictures a giant trout taking the lure. He sees what he hopes to see, but strangely enough the reverse is never true. Never, since man first chiseled a record of his fishing triumphs on a cavern wall in the Paleozoic period, did an angler ever mistake the actual strike of a fish for anything but what it was, and this instance was no exception.

In the precise moment when John, mistaking my order, surged against the paddle and sent the canoe dancing ahead, the forward progress of the bait ceased, and the rod bent slowly and inexorably back. There was no tug or tremor on the line. The rod tip bent in its arc and stayed there without so much as a tell-tale quiver. So far as any physical sign of life was concerned, the bait might have become wedged between two rocks that a harbor dredge could not have moved, but I instinctively knew that I was fast to a good fish.

Instantly there flashed through my mind all the difficulties that I must inevitably face. Were I equipped with a reel of ample capacity and plenty of line, the fly rod would have been able to give a good account of itself in almost any battle, and its springy action would have ultimately worn down a heavy fish, but this patched-up outfit of odds and ends that we had assembled on the spur of the moment was going to further complicate matters that were far too complicated already.

Whimsically, in my moment of need, I thought how easily I could have simplified things if I had only had the forethought to equip myself with a stop-and-go sign, or had at least learned their equivalent in the Montagnais tongue. The coiled line on the reel spool had shrunk to scarcely an inch in diameter and was rapidly growing less. Capable and efficient John, the chap of whom I had boasted so much, had failed me in my moment of greatest need. At this pace the last inch of line would be gone in a few brief seconds, and when the last turn unwound from the spool there would be but one of three things that I might do: I could grasp the rod firmly and leap overboard; I could grasp the canoe firmly and toss the rod overboard, or I could grasp the rod firmly with one hand and the canoe with the other, and watch the line go overboard. Things were rapidly approaching an unpleasant climax and something had to be done. Inspiration seized me. I opened my mouth and yelled "Whoa!" at the top of my voice.

It proved to be the magic word, for John reversed his power and back-paddled so hard that we spun in a slithering circle and abruptly faced back in the direction from which we had come, while I wound hastily in an effort to regain some of the line that I would surely need.

Until that moment there had been no telegraphic communication with the fish, but now a series of little gratings flowed back along the line. The trout had seized the minnow as it passed above him and with its serrated jaws had held it firmly against the steady pull of the line. Now that the pressure was released, he was turning the bait slowly in his mouth so that he might swallow it head first. When that gastronomic feat had been accomplished it would be the correct time to set the hook and begin to pray.

The waiting seemed like minutes; in reality, it was probably but a few seconds. Then there was movement from the depths as the fish turned and started away. I lowered the rod to its limits, then brought it back with every last ounce of power that I dared use. I had timed it right. The barb slid deeply and solidly home, and instantly thereafter things began to happen.

Compared to the fast salmon and the active brook trout, even a big namaycush suffers by comparison, but there is one thing that must be said in his favor. He is imbued with a singleness of purpose that is beyond praise. He has a fixed determination to remain in the element that gave him birth, and he will dig his toenails in and hang on harder than any other fish I know. His distant cousins, the redspot and the salmon, rise to frenzied and sublime heights when hooked, and wear themselves out in their mad effort to free themselves from the restraining thing that holds them fast, but the latter never loses his head and fights a shrewd, defensive battle, resting when a moment's respite is granted him, and doing some wholly unexpected thing at the precise moment when the angler is least prepared to meet it.

This fellow's first reaction to the upward lift of the rod was one of startled surprise. He lunged away, then stopped and shook himself like a dog coming in out of the rain. That expedient failing him, he turned again and swam strongly away.

There was little that I could do about it, except to hold on and give line only as I was forced to, watching meanwhile for a momentary opportunity to free one hand and wave to John to follow the fish. The latter was unnecessary, however, for John had made his one and only mistake in the week that I knew him. He dug in with his paddle and we leaped ahead at a speed that enabled me to regain half a reel of line, and if ever anything is precious in an angler's sight it is those extra coils of line on the reel. As they zip off one by one and near the end, so does despair grip at one's heart. As they come back to fill the spool anew, so does hope return, and all the while one's heart goes bobbing up and down like a monkey on a string.

It is the steady drip of water that wears away the stone, and it is the steady pressure on the rod that wears down a fish. Minutes passed, in which I seemed to be gaining not the least advantage, for the trout still went wherever and whenever he chose, but at last I could feel him weakening. His rushes were still strong but they were noticeably shorter, and there were moments when he lay still and rested and let me recover even more of the cumbersome fly line.

He gave up at last and let me lead him to the surface. Had the reel been large enough to hold the line it would have all been happily over in a few moments, but when it was crowded to its utmost capacity there was still thirty feet left. Laying hold of it just back of the butt guide, I began to strip it carefully in.

Then I saw the fish. He came to the surface, within ten feet of the canoe and rolled weakly. Deep and heavy, he was as long as my arm—a fifteen-pound laker if I ever saw one. John gasped and reached for the net, while I carefully stripped in another yard of line.

Until then, no one could have asked more of luck than it had freely given. Then everything changed in one brief moment. The fish, seeing the outstretched net, gave a last despairing run, a coil of line looped around the reel handle and jammed solidly, the leader twanged tight, then parted like a worn old fiddle string, while the rod sprung straight up and the loose line skittered back to me across the water.

For a moment I sat stunned, and then a sound reached my ears. Softened and muted by the distance. I still knew it for what it was. It was Ernie, giving me a loud and raucous Bronx cheer.

Pan Trout

IF ALL THE derogatory remarks that have ever been hurled at fishermen could be assembled and laid end to end, they would reach from earth to the constellation Pisces. It is of little use to deny such accusations for most of them are true, but I still maintain that credit should be given where credit is due. There is one thing that may be said in favor of the nitwit army of eight millions, who annually travel hundreds of millions of miles and spend hundreds of millions of dollars in their quest for a few slimy and smelly fish. They can accept utter and humiliating defeat with better grace than any other class of people in the world.

The calumnist and the cynic will not agree, but they will say the fisherman excels only because he has had so much practice. Naturally I am of a contrary opinion. I believe that the intimate contact with nature which all fishermen enjoy works a change in the inner man, and makes of him a humbler and wiser person.

There was neither chagrin nor annoyance in our hearts when we conceded the victory to the big lake trout. Our hastily contrived tackle was no match for its power, as another attempt proved. We gave it up then, vowing that some day we would come back, armed with rods and reels and lines that were designed for that sort of thing, and fight it out man to man.

Meanwhile, as long as the wind continued, there was time that must be occupied. We went into a huddle and fired questions at Joe. Where could we find some brook trout? Where was there a stream or small pond that harbored some of those speckled and red-meated fellows of a size to fit conveniently in a frypan?

Joe scratched his head in perplexity for a few moments, then conferred with the Indian, and between them they arrived at a conclusion.

"One mile, maybe," Joe said. "Good place. Hard portage. One hour."

Much might be written about the efficiency of the Indian and part Indian guides in that north country, but one of their greatest virtues is their willingness to work. I have never met but one of their kind who was inclined to shirk. It may be the rigorous climate and the stark necessity of labor that has toughened them to a point where strenuous toil is looked upon as a matter of course, or it may merely be a beautiful willingness to serve, but when one witnesses it just after having left a pampered and motorized younger generation of Americans, the effect is distinctly startling. May I cite one example in proof.

237

We were camped on a salmon lake that lay to the west of the Mistassini. Now in most salmon lakes the quality of water is superb, but here it had a yellowish tint that made us hesitate to use it for drinking purposes. We did not notice anything unusual about the coffee the first morning, but the noon pot of tea had an unusual flavor. I recall wondering if Joe had inadvertently dropped a fish skin in it while he was preparing it, for it had an oily taste, and an aroma that most certainly was not that of lilies of the valley. Thirst conquered me that afternoon and I opened my collapsible cup, dipped it over the side of the canoe and tossed off the contents. I finished my third cupful and was dawdling over the fourth when I tilted it just enough so a ray of sunlight might strike down into its depths. I knew the reason for its peculiar yellowish shade then, for a million diminutive insects played tag and chased each other sportively around in the remaining two tablespoonfuls of liquid. I showed it to the guide but he did not seem to share my aversion. I suppose he was aware of its merits and knew that it was as rich in vitamins as most boardinghouse soups. One could, during a shortage of moose meat, live on it comfortably for a time.

Late that afternoon, and more than two miles from our camp, we passed a sheer, high bluff that rose directly up from the edge of the lake. It was a likely place for a large salmon to be lurking, and we pulled in close to it while I whipped a fly along its edge. Presently I heard the thin trickle of running water, and tracing it to its source I found a tiny rivulet flowing out from a fissure in the rock. We could reach it from the canoe, and as I held my cup beneath it I could feel its icy coolness and see that it was crystal clear.

I said: "We'd better move the camp down here."

The guide shook his head. "No good. No place." He indicated the opposite shore with a wave of his hand. "Much low. Mosquitoes bad. Fly very bad."

"All right," I said resignedly, "but I'd certainly like to be near this water. It's great."

He did not reply, nor did he mention it while we finished the day and paddled home in the gathering dusk, but when I looked out from the tent at daybreak the next morning, one canoe was gone from its place on the shore. The other guide was preparing breakfast, but he shook his head blankly when I asked where Tomo had gone.

"He no say," he answered. "He come back."

I hoped so, and went down to the lake for a morning wash. I was just in time to meet Tomo as he stepped from the canoe. He had the waterpail in his hand and it was filled to the brim with water that was clear and sparkling. He had made the two-mile trip down the lake to the stream we had found, and he did it every morning thereafter for the time we were there; not because anyone asked him to, but merely so that what he considered to be my foolish fancy might be served.

So it was with John the morning to which I have reference. The fact that they had already brought the canoe two miles inland made no difference. He would willingly go another mile, or two, or ten if we signified our desire to do so. We told him to lead on, and away we started.

Bush travel isn't so bad after one becomes used to the weight of the pack and is sufficiently inured to the leaden numbness of tired legs that he can then induce a sort of mental numbness to settle over his mind and can plod on and on with animal fortitude.

239

It was in such a condition that we arrived, an hour later, at a little pond that was hardly a stone's throw across, but our mental lassitude vanished when we saw that the surface was dotted with the wakes of feeding fish. Five minutes later we were out on the pond, our rods assembled and two flies attached to each leader.

There are a few places left where trout abound in all their old-time numbers, and this was one of them. My twain flies had no more than touched the water when a trout was fast to each of them. They were not of a size to write home about or to serve as subjects for pictures to show envious friends, but when they were cleaned and their heads and tails removed they were a per-fect fit in a nine-inch frypan.

I have heard men praise the flavor of hatchery-reared, white-meated, liver-fed trout, but never after they had tasted a native salmon-fleshed brookie. And I know that no trout were ever bet-ter than those we took from that undersized little pond up there in the wilderness. We made several brief trips ashore to dump our offering before John, who was crouching over the fire and rolling the fish back and forth in a bath of sizzling fat. We waited until four plates were heaped high with the golden treasures, and then we went even more hurriedly ashore.

Trail's End

THERE IS ONE THING that I do not like about vacationing. No matter how happy the days, a fellow cannot help looking forward to the time when they must end, and he checks them off regretfully one by one. As the time for departure draws near, each morning has new significance. "Just today and tomorrow," he will say to himself, "and then it will be all over." No matter how strong may be the home ties that bind him, he cannot help but feel a real regret. Each scene becomes newly precious. One no longer merely glances at the white plume of a distant waterfall or the sweeping curve of a hill, but he looks at them long and earnestly, for he is aware that fortune is capricious. He may

promise himself that he will come back again another year to look and love anew, but in his heart he knows that Fate has a way of determining the affairs of men. Other far places will call, other rippling waters will beckon, until these familiar scenes are but a vague and distorted memory.

We knew such a feeling of regret as we packed our duffel for the last time and launched the canoe in the river that led to civilization. How different it was, now that the bow pointed toward the south. On the way in we had paddled eagerly through the smooth stretches, and poled vigorously in the hurrying rapids, chafing at the current that held us back. Now we dipped our blades listlessly, and resented the white water that hurried us onward. Home was beckoning, but we were leaving behind much that we had learned to love.

Still, we had accomplished all that we had hoped, and more. We had not only taken the fighting landlocks from their home waters in the big lake but from several others as well. We had fought the saber-toothed great northern pike in the broad mouth of the Mistassini. We had found the scrappy dore in numberless waters, and had matched our wits against the red-meated square-tails in Commissaires, Otter, Alex, and numberless other lakes. We no longer had the vestige of an excuse for staying. There was nothing to do but go home.

It was late that night when we reached headquarters, but there was a light in the trading room, and we found our outfitter waiting for us there. We bade him goodbye regretfully, for we were planning on a daylight start, but when we told him of it he objected vigorously.

"Non, non," he protested, "I have trip all plan. You like the brook fish, no?"

Ernie's arms were filled with fly-rod cases, nets, and other fishing impedimenta, but now he crossed the room and set them down carefully by the door where they would be handy.

"What did you say?" he asked. "Brook fishing? When? Where? How?"

We started at daylight, just as we had planned, but instead of taking the road that led to the south, we swung westward, and soon we were bumping along over a weedy, grass-grown trail. Where it led we did not know, and neither did we particularly care. It was a new trail, and that was all that mattered.

We came at last to a little clearing where a crude log house braved the wilderness, and there the path ended. Climbing out, we unlashed the canoe and lifted it down, and then, with it balanced once more upon the guide's shoulders, struck off through the tangled spruces.

Presently we heard the murmur that is music to a fisherman's ears—the sound of water rushing down through rocky shallows to form lazy and foam-flecked pools. Trout water! We pushed on hurriedly.

There were trout in the rapids, lusty, hard-hitting trout that had never known the easy existence of rearing pools. But it was not they alone that made the day so perfect; rather, it was because of its unexpectedness.

We had been sentenced to leave it all, and then at the last minute we had been granted a reprieve. What matter if it was only temporary? This day was ours. The song of the waters grew sweeter, the breeze lingered to whisper to us, the birds flitted before us among the branches that overhung the streams, inviting us to follow them on to other hurrying rapids and other quiet pools.

I think, after all, that these are the worthwhile things about fishing, for they linger longest in one's memory. I recall one broad pool below a creaming rapid. I can remember that the moosewood grew close to the banks and that the branches were mangled and broken where a moose had fed on them during the night. I have forgotten whether or not we took a trout from that particular pool, but I can smell again the acid leafmold and the pungent aroma of spruce. I remember that while we sat there quietly in the canoe, a raccoon came unconcernedly down along the narrow fringe of the shore, pounced upon a fat frog that dozed within fifteen feet of us, washed it thoroughly between its almost human front paws, and ate it leisurely there before our eyes.

Yes, these are the things that, all unbidden, came trooping back to whisper in our ears their siren song. "The waters are rippling in the sunshine," they say. "The geese are flying northward, and the wind blows from the south. Come on! It's time to go!"